READY
STEAD
FAME!

The exchange went on, but Coco wasn't listening. One of the music freshmen had stopped by the table with a note for her that had been sent up from the office by Mrs Berg; after unsealing the envelope and reading it through, she simply sat staring at the paper in her hand. Leroy was closest to her, and with no trace of shame he leaned across and read over her shoulder.

Enjoyed the show very much, the note said, *not to mention the chutzpah. If you can act, too, come to my office on Friday and read something for me.* It was signed *Sincerely, – Charles McKay.*

Too stunned to speak right away, Coco handed the note around. When she was finally able to find words, she said, 'It worked! It actually worked!'

Also available in Sphere Books:

THE KIDS FROM FAME II by Lisa Todd
FAME by Leonore Fleischer

The Kids From Fame I

LISA TODD

SPHERE BOOKS LIMITED
30–32 Gray's Inn Road, London WC1X 8JL

First published in Great Britain by
Sphere Books Ltd 1983

TRADE
MARK

Set in Century Schoolbook

Printed and bound in Great Britain by
Cox & Wyman Ltd, Reading

1

For most of his first year at the School of Arts, Bruno Martelli's father had insisted on driving him to school every morning. It was almost an hour's journey through the worst of the downtown traffic that jammed the avenues around East Fifty-Ninth, but Angelo Martelli was a hard man to argue with. Bruno didn't want to seem ungrateful - after all, getting to school by cab did have a certain kind of style about it, even if the meter wasn't running - but it was a fact that, nine times out of ten, he could have made the journey faster on the subway.

It has taken a while, but Bruno had finally managed to lever himself free of the arrangement without actually causing offence. Or so he'd thought; for a few weeks now, his old man had been giving off the quiet signals of a volcano of hurt getting ready to blow. *Oh, Bruno,* he told himself, *you can't get it right for getting it wrong.* He was starting to realise too late that the feedback of pride that his father got from the drive was worth more than the inconvenience to either of them. A simple, direct man, Angelo Martelli had done everything he could to help wind up his son's talent and point him at a target of success. Now it seemed that Bruno was making him into a bystander.

But what could he do? Danny Amatullo had already given him one answer, but it was the same answer that Danny always gave when you cornered him and pressured him into being serious about a real life problem for a while; look inward, analyse it, learn to use it. Bruno shouldn't have been surprised; from Day One since he'd known Danny, Bruno had perceived that the perpetual half-smile and the easygoing, wisecracking manner were only a surface dressing – not a disguise, but the outer shell of a born analyst of human behaviour.

The kind of approach was fine for an actor, Bruno thought as he merged from the IRT into the morning sunlight on Times Square, but as a musician he found the approach more than a little cynical. It didn't seem right to regard his troubles as an almost welcome source of creative fuel, and it didn't seem fair on his father.

But, all the same...

The lights changed from DON'T WALK, and the two crowds on the opposite sides of Forty-Second Street surged towards each other like the armies in some Cecil B. DeMille epic. Bruno slid through them like a fish, bumping and being bumped by nobody, his sheet music hugged under his arm for protection. Forty-Second was looking tired and old; at night it could still dazzle a little with its banks of marquee lights and day-bright sidewalks, but it was only the thin magic of the carnival. The great old theatres had been given over to cinemas, and the cinemas had gone steadily downmarket into skin-flicks and splatter-movie double bills.

New York was a fast town, all right, and since Bruno had started attending the School of the Arts on West Forty-Sixth it seemed that he'd begun to live even faster.

But not fast enough today, it seemed; passing down by the side of the old Rialto Theatre, he could see from a display clock in a shop window full of costume jewellery and dollar jokes that he was late. Coco Hernandez would be up there and waiting already, perhaps Leroy Johnson too; Leroy might be ... well, *relaxed* in some other areas of his lifestyle, but when it came to punctuality for a dance class or a rehearsal he kept better time than a Rolex.

West Forty-Sixth. Bruno was almost running as he turned the corner by the Howard Johnson's, but he kept it down. He had to remember that he was a tousle-haired Italian boy in a sweatshirt, tracksuit top, faded Levis and Ked baseball shoes; he didn't want to arrive at the steps of the school with three cops on his heels all convinced that he'd just mugged some music teacher and stolen his scores.

There it was, an unassuming stone frontage just beyond the Leavitt Building. More than a high school, in no way a dream palace, more like a forge where promise was beaten out into capability with a lot of hard work and sweat. Taking the steps in twos, Bruno smiled. For all the complaints that could be heard around the lunch hall in the middle of the day, almost none of the kids in here was actually being driven. The bait was simply held out to them, the avenues of opportunity indicated, the staff ready to guide and support and point out when a second-best effort had gone by unrecognised.

The bait alone was enough. The bait was accomplishment, achievement, success.

And perhaps also fame.

2

'You're late, man,' Leroy Johnson said as Bruno came in through the dance classroom door. Barely glancing at his friends, he headed straight for the piano and spread his music out on the stand. Coco Hernandez was over by the wall of mirrors, looking just a little cold and fierce, but Bruno knew that this would be frustration rather than anger; Coco was just too small a container to keep so much energy squeezed up inside for long. It looked as if she and Leroy had been spending the time going through their dance number, but it was the song which needed the more work.

'A piano player is late,' Bruno said, running a couple of scales to warm up and get his hands relaxed. 'A pianist is *detained.*' It was a battered old instrument, twice-painted and with none of its castors matching, but the quality of the original tone was still there. He tried a little Chopin, a little Scott Joplin. Bruno had been working on his ARP synthesizer in the basement back home, staying awake until three a.m. to get Coco's arrangement finished, and he always needed a few minutes' practice to make the switch between the types of keyboard.

Coco came around to stand by him, looking over the music. 'Ready when you are, Liberace,' she said, and Bruno winced.

Playing only the right-hand line, he took her through the song. She only needed to hear most of it once, even though there was the muffled sound of Greek bouzouki music from the Dansette record player in the next room as the freshman class groaned through their stretching exercises. Bruno was half-expecting to hear selections from *A Chorus Line* or *Annie* filtering down from Shorofsky's music studio upstairs, but presumably the mid-term auditions that Bruno had seen announced on a blackboard down in the lobby hallway weren't due to start until later.

You had to feel sorry for Shorofsky, sometimes; for years he'd sat through audition after audition where kids without a scrap of real musical talent stood before him and sang *Yesterday*, and now later generations of the same bright-eyed hopefuls were standing up before him and singing *Tomorrow*. Philosophy was his only protection, because sometimes – just *sometimes* – it was possible to turn up some real gold from all the doors. Or to put it another way, as he'd once explained to Julie Miller as she'd bowed her way through a particularly unrewarding set of cello exercises that she'd been given on assignment, if you're hoping to marry a prince then you have to kiss an awful lot of frogs.

'Got it?' Bruno said as he finished the melody line, and Coco nodded. She was frowning slightly, her eyes still on the music, running ahead of Bruno and trying to second-guess some of the technical problems she was likely to hit when it came to the run-through. Watching her at work always reminded Bruno of a demolition team that he'd watched laying dynamite to bring down a Queens tenament block when he'd been six years old. The final effect had been overwhelming, but the real secret had been in the planning and the placing of the charges.

'I got it,' Coco said. 'Let's run it through.'

Leroy had stayed quiet up until now, and he held out a little longer as Coco tried the song, warming into it as she got the mood and the right angle of attack. She didn't drop a note or miss a cue, and even at this early stage it was possible to see the sketchy outlines of what would make an apparently spontaneous performance.

'Coco,' Leroy said as she finished, 'the gig is ours.'

'Leroy,' she said, giving him a narrow look because she *knew* that he was only doing it to provoke her, 'this is not a "gig". This is the International Festival of the Musical Arts.'

'So?' Leroy said, teasing her further.

'So there can only be one lead singer.'

'And who could that be?'

'It better be me.'

You bet, Bruno thought, flipping his score back to the opening for another run-through. *There's one charging tiger I wouldn't care to try stopping.*

★

There was a feeling that Elizabeth Sherwood hadn't been able to shake all morning. She'd even forgotten to come down hard on her junior year English grammar class for making the school record in unreturned mid-trimester papers, and when David Reardon had started to tell her about the role-playing exercise devised by some of his students in which she'd been portrayed as a thinly-disguised Oscar the Grouch giving hell to all of *Sesame Street*, he'd quickly wound up the story on seeing that she was unfocussed and only half-listening.

It wasn't that she couldn't identify the feeling; it was guilt. The tough part was trying to guess why.

At least she knew what had started it. On her way in this morning, not far from the Radio City Music Hall, she'd seen a sight that was hardly a rarity on the streets of Manhattan; a man, presumably homeless, curled up and asleep on one of the metal sidewalk grilles in the shadow of the multimillion-dollar Rockefeller Centre. It was a common enough move practised by bag ladies and modern-day hobos, a way of keeping warm in the updrafts from the sixth avenue subway, and everybody passing by had simply stepped around to give him space. When a cop came along the man would get moved, but until then it was nobody's business.

Elizabeth had glimpsed him for only a moment, hardly paying attention at all. He'd wrapped himself in a black coat, and the heels of his shoes had been worn right down to the nails and beyond.

The only skin showing was on the knuckles that held the coat lapel closed, and just a little of the face that showed from behind that.

Fifty yards or so further down the avenue, she'd started to think about Nick.

She hadn't spoken to her ex-husband in a couple of years, and she had no reason to speak to him now. It was ridiculous. Nick would be doing fine, wherever he'd wound up; that brief image of a wasted life was a common street scene, not an omen. You can't live with someone and not come away with memories of occasional vulnerability, she told herself; Nick could also be strong and extremely self-assertive. In fact, that had been a lot of the problem - two self-assertive characters in such close contact had generated too much heat for comfort.

But still she felt guilty, and she didn't know why. Was it because they'd been out of touch for so long? But that was hardly a reason for guilt - they were *divorced.* Perhaps it was just because she'd made the connection, like the awful feeling she'd had that time after seeing an old lady berating an empty chair in the Chock Full O'Nuts and then having a sudden urge to phone her mother.

It was a riddle. If she couldn't solve it, then she'd have to drive it out of her mind.

Down in the school office, picking up the papers that she'd need to look over before sitting in on the eleven o'clock auditions, she found something that did the job in less than five seconds.

'Worst penmanship I ever saw,' Mrs Berg commented as she handed over the first of the files with its handwritten application form clipped to the front. 'I can barely make out the name. I think it's Phillips, Troy Phillips.'

Elizabeth saw that Mrs Berg was right; the form was almost illegible, and looked more like the work of a six year old than of a child of high school age. She skimmed over the categories once and then, with a sudden jolt of horror, started to read again, more slowly.

'Something wrong?' Mrs Berg said.

It was a moment before Elizabeth could react. 'No,' she began, 'I just recognised . . .' but then she let it tail away. 'Excuse me,' she said, and she gathered up the form and the files and headed out of the office.

There was a telephone free in the faculty lounge. Checking against the address on Troy Phillips' application form, Elizabeth looked up the Phillips number in the Manhattan Central directory that spent most of its time holding up one corner of a broken coffee table. She dialled, and waited. She had to do this, she told herself. She had to make sure that her first reaction had been a mistake.

After a few moments, the phone was lifted. 'Phillips,' a woman's voice said.

'*Helen* Phillips?' Elizabeth said with a sinking feeling, knowing now that there was no mistake.

'That's right. Who's this?'

'It's me, Helen, Elizabeth Sherwood. Remember?'

3

Bruno had run the song through with Coco four times over, but then they'd had to break at ten-thirty for Coco's voice class. Leroy was already saying that the Festival was in the bag, but Coco wasn't allowing herself to be so confident. Bruno was going to say nothing until his opinion was asked, and at this early stage he wasn't even sure that he *had* an opinion. The most that he had was a feeling; a feeling that something, somewhere was missing.

But that was crazy. He'd been working on the arrangement until his head buzzed, and until he got some of his perspective back he was probably the last person to be making judgements. Keep your mouth shut, Bruno, and play.

Actually, there was one more thing he had to do; Buffy's Music Store hadn't yet come through with a Ligeti score that he'd had to order, and it was time for a phone call. They'd taken his money happily enough, after all. Digging in his pocket for change, Bruno made for one of the nearby corridor pay phones.

Alongside the phones were some plastic chairs, old office throwouts; sitting on one of these was a kid that Bruno didn't recognise. He was about seventeen, and so neatly turned out that his presence could only mean one thing; he was here for the auditions.

'Got change for a dollar?' Bruno asked, bringing out a couple of crumpled bills and no coins. The kid looked up, momentarily caught off-balance.

'I have two quarters and two dimes and three nickles and I have to keep it,' he said, all of a piece as if he'd been drilled in what he had to say.

Bruno shrugged. 'Okay,' he said. I wouldn't want to deprive you. I can make the call later.'

Now the kid looked puzzled, and Bruno suddenly felt just a little bit mean. He remembered his own first day in the school, apprehensive and more bewildered than he'd care to admit even now, sitting with his appointment card and wondering whether the next couple of hours was going to decide the course of his whole life. He said, 'You're auditioning?'

'At eleven.'

'You've got another twenty minutes to wait.'

'Twenty-two,' the kid said without any obvious glance at the corridor clock. 'I have twenty-two minutes.'

Bruno gave him what he hoped was a reassuring smile. 'Nervous?'

The kid swallowed hard, and then nodded. Bruno went on, 'What's your speciality?'

He looked down, fumbled at some sheets on the chair beside him, and then held up the papers for Bruno to see. They were piano parts for songs, much-used and repaired with Scotch tape. A couple were photocopies.

'Ah,' Bruno said encouragingly, 'an *afficionado*. That's my thing. Music.'

'I sing,' the kid said, and then added, 'and I play the guitar sometimes.'

'I compose,' Bruno said, and he put out his hand to shake. 'The name's Bruno Martelli.'

'Very pleased to meet you,' the kid said formally, taking Bruno's hand and giving it one brief shake. 'My name is Troy, Troy Phillips.'

'Well hello, Troy Phillips. Want to take a twenty minute tour?'

'Now I only have nineteen...'

'Okay, okay,' Bruno said quickly. 'I'll make it as fast as I can.'

As they did a quick turn around the music rooms and the dance studios, Bruno watched the boy and tried to make some kind of guess on how he was likely to do. It was impossible. Even for seventeen he seemed . . . well, *unmarked* was the only word that Bruno could think of to describe it, and he was sure that a lot of what he was saying wasn't even being fully understood. Nothing in the books said that a musician had to be a particularly social animal - but it helped, it certainly helped. Especially in a high-pressure community like the School of the Arts.

'Now,' Bruno said as they got close to three-seventeen, the room where Benjamin Shorofsky would be waiting to hear Troy Phillips sing, 'when you audition, keep a low profile.'

'Low profile?'

'Never point out the error of the old guy's ways. Especially if you're not into classical.' Not a good move, Bruno, he thought immediately when he saw the look on Troy's face, and so he did his best to make it up by adding, 'Never mind. He'll like you because you're quiet and polite.'

'Doesn't he like you?'

'Shorofsky?' Bruno said, thinking of the way that Shorofsky had screwed up his face in an expression of exquisite agony when Bruno had played him a short synthesizer work that he called *Edvard Münch; A Howling in the Void.* 'He's crazy about me. He just has trouble expressing his feelings.' They came level with three-seventeen; just another door to Bruno, but something rather more awesome for Troy. 'Well, break a leg.'

Again, Troy looked blank. 'Why would I do that?'

'You never heard anybody say 'break a leg' before?'

'I don't want to hurt myself. I just want to be in this school.'

'It's old showbiz talk. Means . . . good luck.'

Troy brightened. 'Thank you.'

'Pleasure.' To get the kid over his first hurdle, Bruno knocked on the door and heard Ben Shorofsky call out in reply. Troy opened up, and walked in to the first part of his audition.

Bruno shook his head as he walked away. Strange kid. *Strange* kid.

★

Although there were kitchens and a hot-food counter in the school, lunch in the teachers' lounge mostly meant a rearrangement of the furniture and the production of a lot of paper bags. It wasn't exactly five-star cuisine, but then the chipped tables and chairs and the State Education Board regulation decor weren't exactly five-star, either.

Lydia Grant watched Dave Reardon with a kind of awe. She'd pulled a velour top over her leotard and her dark curls were still back in a band after the morning's dance session. There was a hunk of cheese and an apple on the table before her, but they seemed insignificant alongside the young drama teacher's spread; in the space between them he'd lined up a monstrous Hero sandwich, two bowls of veggies, chips, soup, and a drink.

'It's fuel food,' he explained when he saw the look that Lydia was giving him. 'Gives me stamina for Danny Amatullo. He's in love, and it's wearing me out.'

It seemed that Danny had, in his own kind of way, flipped over a pretty, soft-featured blonde in his class named Diana Huddleston. All of his best-tried approaches had got him nowhere, but in the end he'd scored by getting Doris Schwartz to draft his dialogue. Diana was being won over, and the story was gradually getting around the school. When it finally reached Diana, Danny was going to have to watch out.

Lydia moved over to make way for Ben Shorofsky, just arrived and pushing his way through the chairs towards them. She said, 'What wears *me* out is thinking about these auditions for the music festival.'

'One less thing for the drama department to worry about,' Reardon said. He took a huge bite out of his sandwich and then sat back, gopher-cheeked and smirking.

'Biggest thing will be to come up with a lead singer,' Lydia said. 'Rules say we can enter a whole show, but there can only be one lead singer. None of you tell that child, but I think Coco has it wrapped up.'

'Wrapped up?' Shorofsky said as he lowered himself to sit beside Lydia, for once not complaining about the uncivilised height of the chairs or the embarrassing noises that the vinyl padding always made. 'I wouldn't say it was wrapped up. Not after eleven this morning, anyway.'

There was one space left in the circle, one body needed to close the customary group; the body was Elizabeth Sherwood's, and she was over at the coffee-maker helping herself.

Lydia said, 'Eleven o'clock? What's the magic about eleven o'clock?'

'Because,' Shorofsky said with a certain pride, 'that's when a new boy auditioned. Sings like a dream.'

Reardon was finally fit to speak again. 'I take it we have a new student?'

'Immediately. His name's Troy Phillips. He's got a wonderful voice, very special.'

Elizabeth was with them. Nobody immediately noticed that she'd left her coffee standing untouched. 'Special is a good word,' she said, and Lydia looked up at Elizabeth. There was something in the way she spoke that Lydia couldn't identify. A trace or irony ... or even a certain bitterness?

Shorofsky said, 'You know the boy?'

'I know his parents,' Elizabeth said, and she sat. 'Mister Shorofsky, didn't you notice anything... peculiar about Troy?'

Shorofsky thought for a moment, and then shook his head. 'He's shy,' he began, but then he couldn't think of anything else to add.

'Did you ask about his background? Where he's gone to school?'

'Come to think of it . . . when I asked him, he simply began to sing again. After that, I guess I forgot to ask.'

Elizabeth looked at the floor for a moment. 'He was afraid you wouldn't accept him if you knew the truth.'

Shorofsky leaned forward. 'Nothing he could say would change my mind. In a world of mediocrity, this boy is an exception.'

'I'm afraid you're right,' Elizabeth said, meeting each gaze in turn. 'That boy with the "wonderful voice" already attends a special school . . . with other "special" children.'

‘What do you mean,’ Shorofsky said cautiously, ‘special?’

Elizabeth hesitated for a moment, but there was no hiding it. The truth was going to come out sometime, and then all of the prejudices and the misplaced good intentions were going to be flying back and forth like bees from a busted hive.

‘In a less enlightened age,’ she said, ‘the term was “retarded”.’

4

Retarded. A label, a classification, a buzzword. Shorofsky argued for Troy Phillips, and Shorofsky won; as far as *he* was concerned the term simply didn't apply to a boy who may even have had an edge in talent and ability on anyone else in the school. To turn him down, for any reason, would be an act - and here Shorofsky thundered, his clenched fist held dramatically aloft - of criminal folly.

Nobody saw him wink at Dave Reardon afterwards. But even though the act was calculated, the effect was one hundred per cent sincere. Shorofsky wanted the boy in his class, in his care; and he got him. The papers were processed through, and Troy Phillips took his seat in the music class between Bruno Martelli and Coco Hernandez on the next Wednesday morning.

A few curious glances were thrown his way, but Troy simply sat with his pencils arranged neatly on the desk and his hands folded before him. He said hello to Bruno, and although he didn't say much else it was easy to see that he was burning with pride.

Shorofsky came in with a stack of papers, which he split into two piles and gave to the nearest students to hand out. 'As your exams are returned,' he said drily, 'you may experience a wave of nausea...'

A wave of nausea was duly experienced by the class. Coco Hernandez groaned aloud when she saw her grade.

'Apparently,' Shorofsky went on, 'the subject of harmony failed to capture your enthusiasm. Let's hope the situation's changed by Friday, when you have another exam on this material.'

Bruno sighed when he got his own paper back. It was the usual story; a flawless grasp, terribly expressed. In academic work, his keyboard skills tended to show up rather less well than his bad habits.

Shorofsky was by now behind his desk and lowering himself to sit in his swivel chair. 'Luckily for you all,' he said, 'we can begin preparing almost immediately. First I should like to introduce a new student, Troy Phillips.' Troy made an intent study of the desk before him, knowing that everyone would be looking his way. 'Mister Phillips is a very fine singer indeed, and I invite you to hear him at your earliest possible convenience.' He winked at Troy, much as he'd winked at Dave Reardon a few days before. 'It will be worth it. And now, if we can all turn to page fifty-four...'

'How 'bout right now?' Coco cut in, after a quick glance at the uninviting weight of the harmony textbook on the desk in front of her.

Shorofsky looked up, momentarily jolted from

his track. 'Excuse me?'

'How about if he sings a song for us now?'

'But what of our rules of harmony?'

There was a faint and slightly desperate rumbling from the whole of the class. Right now, *anything* would be preferable to the rules of harmony.

'Mister Shorofsky,' Bruno said, with a grin that told Shorofsky that one of the darts had been stolen from his own quiver and was about to be used against him, 'the basic rules of harmony have been with us for centuries, long before today's fickle musical styles and they will be here for many . . .'

Shorofsky made resigned damping motions with his hands, as if he was trying to push back an irresistible tide in the certain knowledge of failure. 'I get the gist,' he said. 'Well, if the rest of the class is willing to postpone the inevitable . . .'

The rest of the class showed its feelings in a roar of approval as Bruno and Troy made their way up towards the piano.

'What do you want to sing?' Bruno said as he got himself seated.

'Do you know *Penny Lane*?'

'Sure.'

Bruno vamped an introduction, and Troy launched in. It was a nervous start, but within a couple of bars he'd found confidence. Shorofsky leaned back in his chair and watched; he watched Troy, and he watched the reaction of the music class.

It was as he'd known it would be. Troy was

knocking them dead with a powerhouse performance – all shyness gone, all uncertainty forgotten, he was transformed. *Retarded*, Shorofsky thought angrily. Well, it all depended on your criteria. How typical of the modern world – when we fail people, we invent a label and make out that they've failed *us*.

Shorofsky let his attention drift to Coco Hernandez. What he saw there was a reaction that differed slightly from that of the others. She was recognising Troy as an exceptional singer, but there was something else, a slightly feral quality in her eyes that told Shorofsky that she was identifying a threat of some kind.

A little competition would do her talents no harm at all; it all depended on how she handled it. Coco's position as the 'best' of the singers at the School of the Arts had been assured for too long, and Shorofsky had noticed that it had taken some of her edge away; unconsciously echoing Bruno Martelli's thought of the week before, he'd begun to feel that there was something missing in her attack. Instead of feeding on her own hunger, she was starting to sound just a little like some facelifted old crooner on her tenth farewell tour.

Well, perhaps that was unfair. But Troy was making her think hard, and that was good. As for Troy himself, he was bringing the song to an end in grand style. A little too much John Lennon and not enough Troy Phillips perhaps, but that was natural and it was nothing that wouldn't be overcome.

Bruno hit the last chord, Troy ended the last note cleanly, and the music class leapt to its feet. The kids crowded around the piano, swamping Troy in a sudden wave of enthusiasm and appreciation, and Shorofsky was satisfied to see that Coco Hernandez was right there in the middle of them. He watched the backslapping and the handshaking with an indulgent smile - but then his smile slowly died.

Troy was getting anxious, seeing faces crowding up on all sides and finding no way out. Shorofsky tried to speak, but the noise was too much for him to be heard. Troy was struggling for control. He looked longingly towards the door. Someone's hand grabbed his shoulder, and started to shake.

That was it. Troy broke free, roughly forcing his way past four or five astonished students. He tripped and almost stumbled, but he recovered his balance. He'd gone from the room before anyone knew what had happened.

There were blank looks, stunned faces. The chatter had abruptly become an uncomprehending silence. Shorofsky knew exactly what had happened, but he knew that he couldn't explain it.

'He's ... very shy,' he said, which wasn't entirely untrue. 'I think you overwhelmed him. Please fend for yourselves until I return.'

He went after Troy, and caught up with him no more than fifty yards away. The boy was muttering something that sounded like, *She was right, she was right.* He gave a start when Shorofsky gently touched him on the shoulder.

'Who was right, Troy?' Shorofsky said.

'Mother... said to stay.'

'Stay where, Troy?'

The boy took a couple of deep breaths. He was starting to get his control back, but his nervous glance at a couple of drama seniors going by on their way to the lockers told Shorofsky that he was afraid of being overheard.

Shorofsky looked around. The nearby classrooms were all in use, but there was a walk-in supply closet cross the corridor.

'Step into the office,' Shorofsky said, and he led Troy over.

Once inside, with the musty smells of chalk and new paper, Shorofsky switched on the overhead light and closed the door. Troy said, 'Can you keep a secret, Mister Shakof...'

'I can,' Shorofsky said quickly, to avoid any extra awkwardness.

'Tight?'

Shorofsky nodded.

'I go to another school, too. You won't tell?'

'I won't tell.'

'It's a school for kids like me. I'm not...' Troy motioned vaguely, back in the direction of the classroom. 'I'm not like those kids. I'm different. I won't ever be like those kids. They're better than me.'

'I don't think that's true,' Shorofsky said firmly.

'At the other school, they're all like me. At that school, *I'm* better.' He looked at the floor, sorrowfully. 'It was a mistake. I made a mistake. I'll go back. I...'

'No,' Shorofsky said. 'You didn't make a mistake. You did a very brave thing, and I have the greatest respect for you.' Troy calmed a little. Shorofsky went on, 'Listen to me. Next month there will be a very important music festival. I would like you to be the lead singer representing this school. Will you stay?'

Troy looked up. Shorofsky saw disbelief, hope, the glint of a single crystal tear. Troy was back from the edge.

But Shorofsky was now walking dangerously close to it.

The reaction down in the teachers' lounge was just as Shorofsky had been expecting; disbelief, incredulity, and a certain amount of apprehension.

'He was going to leave the school,' Shorofsky insisted. Lydia Grant and Elizabeth Sherwood were both looking dubious; Dave Reardon seemed to be thinking something over. 'I had to do something!'

Reardon said, 'I thought the whole idea behind "mainstreaming" was to treat him like any other kid?'

'Do the other kids know about this yet?' Lydia added.

Shorofsky shook his head. 'No, I...'

'Well, when they find out, I'd give some serious thought to hiring a bodyguard.'

'It's easy for all of you,' Shorofsky protested. 'Is he taking dance? No.' He turned to Elizabeth, who had been listening but who so far had said nothing. 'Is he taking English? No.' Now Reardon. 'Is he taking drama?'

'Yes,' Reardon said promptly, which stopped the conversation in its tracks for a moment.

'David,' Elizabeth said gently, 'he barely reads.'

'But he *can* read,' Reardon pointed out. 'Acting is acting. Reading is reading. Drama might just build his confidence.'

'And it might tear him apart. It can tear *anybody* apart.'

But Reardon had obviously thought it through. 'One thing's for sure, this kid's got guts. And if he wants to be treated like every other kid, I say give him a real chance. Not some kind of . . . free ride.'

Now Elizabeth was getting really worried. She turned to Shorofsky. 'Benjamin,' she said, 'it does seem to go against everything we wanted for Troy.'

Shorofsky took a breath, and looked at each of them. 'You're all right, every one of you. In the long run, I suspect that I may be guilty of a slight error in judgement. But –' And here he looked directly at Elizabeth, not in accusation but more in appeal – 'I would like to have seen any one of you listen to that frightened voice, and look into those confused eyes, and do anything different.'

And then, in silence, he turned and walked out of the lounge. His problems weren't over. Even if there wasn't some kind of explosion when he went public about the cancelled auditions, there were going to be questions; questions that he wasn't sure how to handle.

He could stall it for a couple of days. No more.

5

Come Friday, Bruno thought that he was going to be late again; his train was stopped for an eerie ten minutes in the Queensborough tunnel under the East River as IRT guards checked the track ahead after a driver's report that he'd seen somebody running through the darkness. In the end, the backup had been so heavy that they'd restarted the trains. If there *was* anyone sneaking around down there, he'd be brought out the quick and easy way, flattened across the front of a midtown express.

Ten minutes had somehow managed to stretch themselves out into a half-hour by the time that Bruno made it to Forty-Sixth. He'd all but missed his first class - Sherwood was really going to crack the whip over him for this. Even on the slowest days riding in the back of the cab, he'd never been so late that he couldn't sprint that last couple of blocks and dash up the stairs to dive in just as the door was being closed.

Perhaps he ought to speak to his father again... but no, no, forget that. The subject had been closed too firmly the last time, and Bruno couldn't see any way of opening it up again.

Well, there was no point in hurrying now; better to

miss the class completely than to attempt to sidle in halfway through. Maybe he'd even get by unnoticed – although he didn't think he had much chance of that. Sherwood remembered skipped classes like other people remembered football scores.

He walked out of the dust and the heat and the noise of the street into the dust and the heat and the comparative silence of the school's main entrance hall. There was some new stuff on the music noticeboard, Bruno saw immediately; Ben Shorofsky was just walking away with a box of pins and a couple of out-dated posters in his hand. He didn't look Bruno's way; he seemed to be in a hurry. Bruno was about to cross the hall and check the board, when he saw Troy Phillips.

Troy was just arriving, his sack lunch in his hand. He didn't have the desperate look of a latecomer, and he didn't seem to be in any big hurry. Bruno waited for him.

'You just getting in?' Bruno said, but Troy didn't seem to hear the question.

'I've got a drama class today,' he said. 'I spent all last night learning the scene. I know all the words, both parts.'

'You have some kind of weird schedule?' Bruno said. 'I never see you in English or Chemistry, or –'

'I don't have to take those classes,' Troy said, and Bruno's eyes widened. There must be a way out, some kind of scheme that Troy knew. The big question was, could Bruno get in on it too? *Anything* that got people out from under Sherwood was going to be in big demand.

'What's the secret?' he said.

'I don't have a secret,' Troy said. 'I have tutors.'

The distant, far-off sound was the crashing of Bruno's hopes. 'Tutors?'

'Special tutors.'

Bruno wanted to ask more, but the end-of-period bell drowned him out for a moment. Doors were slamming open, and the hall was suddenly filled with a flash-flood of bodies.

'You see,' Troy explained, raising his voice to be heard and clutching at his lunchbag as they were buffeted by the tide, 'I got behind in my grades because I was sick and missed a year.'

Bruno heard *I don't believe this* from over by the music notice board, and when he looked over he saw that a big crowd had gathered around Shorofsky's latest announcement. Whatever it said, it was causing a stir. Coco Hernandez was pushing her way towards them, and she seemed angry.

Bruno wondered what he could have done to make himself into a target; but he quickly realised it wasn't him that Coco was aiming for.

'You know,' she said to Troy, 'for somebody that's supposed to be shy, you sure must know some smart moves.'

Troy looked around, stunned. He hadn't been expecting this. 'Excuse me?'

'No, I don't think I will.'

'Coco,' Bruno said, 'What's going on?'

Coco turned to him. 'A notice just went up. The

singing auditions for the festival are off.'

'I didn't ask them to do that,' Troy said quickly.

'Well, you must have done something!'

Bruno tried to bring a little calm. He felt as if he'd walked into the middle of a story where he knew nothing of what was going on around him. He said, 'Coco, why are the auditions off?'

'Because they've already made their choice.'

Oh-oh. Even though he could guess the answer, Bruno said, 'Who is it?'

Coco's gaze on Troy was like a finely-tuned laser. 'I think you ought to ask your friend.'

Troy seemed to get smaller. 'I'll be late for drama class,' he said weakly, and then after a half-second's hovering he took off so fast that he simply seemed to vanish. Bruno started to call after him, but it was too late.

He looked at Coco. She hadn't been expecting this; she was defensive, defiant.

'I'm sorry,' she said, 'but it's just not fair. I had to say something.'

'Feel better?' Bruno said.

6

After Troy's drama class, everybody knew.

The scene that brought it all out was a two-hander that Reardon had assigned to Troy and Doris Schwartz. Troy had been proud of the fact that he'd managed to learn both parts, but this proved to be his downfall; even though it was only an unblocked rehearsal, he saw the faces of his watching classmates and from the very opening was subject to performance nerves. He took Doris's lines by mistake, prompted her when she paused, and forgot his stage directions.

Dave Reardon could see a disaster in the making, and knew that it had been a mistake to put Troy on the spot so early. But what else could he have done? The whole point of the move had been to bring Troy more into the circle of the school, not to single him out for a lighter load that would make him conspicuous and set him apart.

So Reardon told them to relax, take it from the top again and use their scripts, and this was another mistake. Troy couldn't find his place, and it slowly became obvious that it was because he simply couldn't get the words; the harder he tried, the harder it got. Finally he just froze. Reardon moved the class along, but it was too late. Troy said nothing for the rest of the lacklustre session, and he left before anyone could speak to him.

Bruno found him sitting on the hall steps. He wasn't in tears or upset, but he was as alone as it's ever possible to be.

'Hey,' Bruno said, sitting alongside him and forcing himself to be bright, 'you're going to be late for music.'

'I can't go to music,' Troy said.

'Why not? You belong there.'

'No. I don't belong in music.' Troy looked around the stairway. 'I don't belong in this school.'

'Troy,' Bruno said carefully, 'you have talent. A lot of talent.'

'I *have* a place to sing,' Troy said evenly, as if he'd thought it through and was facing the facts. 'It's a special group. For the educationally handicapped.' He'd almost managed to keep it out, but the bitterness started to come through on the last words.

'That's okay,' Bruno said, 'but I think you want more than that.'

Troy shook his head. 'It's the kids in this school ... I don't know how to act with them.'

'Why not just be you?'

'Because I'm not good enough. They're perfect, they're normal.'

'Troy, perfect and normal are two different things, believe me.'

'Well,' Troy said, as if it was a matter that only perfect and normal people could ever dismiss so lightly, 'I'll never be either.' He got to his feet. 'I don't belong here. I belong in the Chase School for the Educationally Handicapped.' Without looking back and without saying goodbye, he walked down the stairs.

'Hey,' Bruno said, 'Hey, Troy, wait a minute!'

But Troy was already across the hall and on his way out of the door.

Watching herself in the dance studio mirror, Coco Hernandez could see the dance teacher coming around behind her. Lydia Grant stopped at Coco's place in the line and watched for a few moments, and the reflection showed that she wasn't exactly thrilled by what she was seeing.

'Coco,' she said, 'you're asleep.'

Coco lost the beat, tried to pick it up again. She got it wrong and almost tripped Leroy, who was working next along in the line.

'Child,' Lydia said, 'you're dancing with rocks in your feet.'

'I'm doing my best, Miss Grant.'

'Honey, I've seen your best. And that ain't it.' Lydia looked down the line; the distraction was taking effect, and one or two of the others were falling out of step. 'Okay,' she said, 'two-minute breather.'

The line instantly collapsed, and the dancers sank to the floor. As the teacher went across to end the music, Leroy tried to get a reading on Coco.

'That's a drag about Troy,' he said, watching her. 'His folks took him out of school this morning.'

Coco, leaning back on her elbows and breathing hard, looked up in surprise. 'Why?'

Leroy shrugged. 'Now they'll have to set up the festival auditions all over again.' Coco was frowning. 'Well, now you've got a shot at it. Isn't that what you wanted?'

'I wanted a shot at it,' she said frowning harder. 'But not this way.'

She went looking for Bruno Martelli; after all, Bruno had been the one who'd more or less taken Troy under his wing, shown him around, introduced him to people. Nobody had seen Bruno for a while, but Danny Amatullo suggested that she should try around the drama studio or the dressing rooms. Bruno had been assigned the part that Troy had so spectacularly blown, and he and Doris Schwartz were probably working on it together in order to have it ready for the next session. Danny, meanwhile, had his own problems; his wooing of Diana Huddleston had been going fine until pressure of work had forced Doris to call a halt to his supply of matinee-idol dialogue. Thrown back on his own inventions, he wasn't doing half so well.

Coco looked in on the drama studio, but it was occupied by a freshman class lying on the scuffed floor and pretending that they were hovering inches above it as Reardon strolled around the gaps between them and talked them through. Even *he* looks sick about this whole business, Coco thought, and she went to check the dressing rooms.

The dressing rooms were empty, but there were voices coming from makeup next door.

'What gets me,' she heard Bruno saying, 'is that of all the schools, we should have been the one to accept him.'

'We tried.' The second voice belonged to Doris Schwartz. Coco hesitated, not wanting to eavesdrop, not wanting to butt in, unable to turn around and walk away.

'You call what we did trying?' Bruno was saying. 'We find out the guy has a disability, and we treat him like a freak. Then Coco completely flips out over the audition.'

At the sound of her own name, Coco knew that she couldn't wait outside any longer. She pushed open the door and stepped through.

Bruno and Doris were at the far end of the room, sitting in the fairground glare thrown by the lightframes of the makeup mirrors. Their backs were towards Coco, their playbooks open and unread before them. Doris said, 'Let's face it, none of us handled this thing the way we should have. None of us.'

They both gave a little jump as Coco spoke.

'But I'm the one who made him feel like he didn't belong,' she said. 'I'm the one who hurt him.'

7

The Chase school was, it seemed, a place where teachers and assistants handled every kind of handicap that came their way. Coco found the address in the phonebook, and she set out in her lunch hour on the next day to walk the couple of miles it would take her to get there. She could have taken the subway, but she wanted time to think. She'd been thinking hard for most of the previous day and partway through the night, but she hadn't found a sure way around her problem yet.

She passed four or five men sitting on the stoop before a brownstone, all of them having a small street-party of their own with beers and spirits in brown paper bags that were passed from hand to hand. Empty beer cans had been set neatly on the stone posts, and the pavement before them was dark with runoff water from an unclosed faucet. They whistled and shouted as Coco went by. She didn't even seem to hear them.

When she got to the school, she stopped outside. The wheelchair ramp up to the main door told her that she was about to step into new territory. She was suddenly, unaccountably nervous, and she was ashamed for it. She walked through the main door and up to the school clerk's desk, and she asked if it would be possible to speak to Troy Phillips.

The clerk sent her to wait in an open area, a patio surrounded by classroom buildings. Some of the kids that she saw passing through were in wheelchairs, some had disabilities that were immediately visible, but most looked . . . well, *ordinary*.

She tried to relax a little. She didn't even hear Troy coming up beside her.

'They said you wanted to see me,' he said.

Coco looked up at him. There was something slightly different about him, as if he'd been building protective walls around himself and doing it in such a hurry that the cracks still showed. But there was also something else; a sense of relief, a feeling akin to that of the fox when he gets back amongst his own kind and away from the danger of the hounds.

'Sit down,' she invited, but Troy shook his head. Coco got to her feet, and they walked the length of the patio.

It wasn't easy to find an opening. 'Troy,' she began, 'everybody misses you. Bruno, Doris, Leroy...'

'I don't want to hear,' Troy said.

'I miss you, too.'

Troy stopped, and looked at her. What was she trying to pull? 'You hurt me,' he pointed out. It wasn't an accusation, just a statement of fact.

'I know,' Coco said, 'and I'm sorry. I want a chance to make it up to you.'

But Troy was already shaking his head. 'This is

where I belong,' he said. 'This is where I can be on top of the hill instead of right down at the bottom. No place else.'

'It'll stay that way, if you never try.'

'I did try. I'd rather stay here.'

'I want you to come back. Shorofsky's holding new auditions.'

There was a moment's hesitation, but no more. 'If I come back and if they let me sing . . . well, we'll all know why, won't we?'

'Not this time, Troy. If you win, it'll be because of your heart and your voice. I can handle that if you can.'

'You don't understand,' Troy began, but Coco understood only too well.

'I understand you're scared,' she said. 'But you're not alone in that. Every time I get up to sing or to dance, I'm sure the audience will see me shaking.'

'It's different for you.'

'It comes with the territory. If you're going to perform, you're going to be scared. You don't have a corner on stage fright, just because you're "different".' Coco smiled, to take any of the sting out of what she was saying.

'But I'm . . .'

'I know what you are. You're a singer, and that's what counts.'

She'd gone as far as she could; anything beyond that was up to Troy himself. She wanted to see him at the audition, even if his presence increased the pressure on her own chances, because she'd already made herself face the fact that she'd been trying to put over to Troy; coming out first wouldn't mean a thing to either of them if the competition itself wasn't the best on offer.

She moved to leave. Troy called after her, 'What happens when it's over?'

She grinned at him, walking backwards. 'You'll be on unemployment like the rest of us. That's showbiz!'

She gave him one last wave, and left. Over to you, Troy.

The story of Danny Amatullo's coaching had finally reached Diana Huddleston. Now almost everybody in the school was waiting for them to meet up again. Some were laying bets on which eye she'd black; others were only laying bets on which eye she'd black first. They were hoping to be around when it happened, but preferably at a safe distance.

The way that it turned out, the Big Event took place in a quiet corner of the library with nobody watching.

Diana was having to put in some extra time on her Spanish, because she'd been caught out over a passage from *Don Quixote* only the day before, Ms Ramirez had pointed out in a marginal note to Diana's class paper that her summary of the book's theme bore an uncanny resemblance to the sleeve notes on the *Man of La Mancha* cast recording in the school's record collection. A little extra sweat, please, Huddleston.

So Diana sat on her own with a large stack of books disguising a quick-study aid booklet that she'd bought from the Barnes and Noble bookstore on Broadway, and she tried to get absorbed. It didn't help that she kept humming *The Impossible Dream* to herself, over and over.

When Danny arrived, he made straight for her.

She was startled; not so much by his sudden appearance, but by the fact that he came at her with a full head of steam. *He* was the one who ought to be cowering in the corner with his arms held up over his head as he cried for mercy!

'I have nothing to say to you,' Diana said quickly, but Danny kept on coming.

'That's great,' he said, because I've got enough to say for the both of us.' He pulled out a chair and sat himself down beside her. And then, in a kind of token deference to the fact that they were in a library, he lowered his voice just a little. 'First of all,' he said, 'all that moon, June, spoon stuff wasn't me. Doris Schwartz wrote all those lines. I just delivered them.'

'I know. It's the dumbest thing I ever heard.'

'What was dumb is that you went for it.'

'I certainly did not,' Diana began to protest, but Danny cut in.

'Lock, stock, and barrel,' he said flatly. 'You went for the words, Diana, instead of me. Maybe when I talk it doesn't sound like Shakespeare or even Doris Schwartz, but I had feelings for you. Real feelings.'

Diana was still gaping at the intensity of his approach as he stood up to leave. After a couple of steps, he stopped and turned to face her.

'But do you want to know what's even dumber?' he said. "That I even tried it in the first place. *That* was dumb. Next time, the kid is going to trust the kid. Period.'

With that, he walked off. He didn't even give her time to reply. Seconds later, the library doors banged closed.

'Do you think I let him off too lightly?' Diana said, to no-one in particular.

8

There was a high turnout for the Festival auditions on the following Tuesday. The roll-call of potential singers was a long one, but only eight people had put themselves forward as serious contenders for the lead spot. Coco was drawn to audition second. On the list in the main hall, she saw that Troy Phillips had been drawn to sing seventh.

Bruno accompanied her, as before, and she stood on the bare stage in the main hall of the School of the Arts and gave it everything. When it was over, Shorofsky thanked her from the almost-empty auditorium; Coco shaded her eyes against the working lights in the hope that she might be able to get some idea of the music professor's reaction, but he was giving nothing away. Up at the back, a few students were waiting for their turn to come around. Troy Phillips was there, sitting a little way apart. He smiled at her, and half-waved.

Coco let herself smile back, and then she and Bruno withdrew to the wings to make way for the next soloist and her keyboard player. As soon as they were offstage, she said, 'Well? What'd you think?'

'I think you're a wonderful singer,' Bruno said

diplomatically, and Coco could tell immediately that he was stalling.

'You think I'll get it?' she said.

'I can't tell you how glad I am that I don't have to make that decision.'

'I know, Bruno, but it's your song. What do you think?'

'I think you should ask Leroy.'

'Leroy? Why?'

'Because he's a better liar than I am.'

'You don't have to lie. It was bad?'

'No,' Bruno said, 'it wasn't bad. It was wonderful.'

'I don't understand you.' Coco was starting to get angry. 'What are you trying to say?'

They came down the backstage steps, and Bruno pushed open the fireproof door to the dressing-room corridor. 'What I'm saying is that you're a wonderful singer, but not every song is right for you. Yehudi Menuhin's a great violinist, but when he duets with Grapelli he sounds as stiff as a board. I try to write a cantata, and it sounds like a McDonald's commercial.'

'You think Troy's a better singer,' Coco said, getting right through to the heart of it.

'For this particular song, yes,' Bruno conceded. 'For another song, who knows?'

Coco sighed heavily, and didn't put up a fight. Bruno said, after a moment, 'You okay?'

'It hurts.'

'I know. But can you handle it?'

'I'll find a way,' Coco said.

★

Most days before a class, Benjamin Shorofsky could be found setting up the blackboard in the music room. It saved time during the lesson, and time was one of the scarcest commodities in the drum-tight School of the Arts schedule. Coco went along a little early, hoping he'd be alone. She'd told Bruno that she'd find a way to handle the hurt, but she felt that she was going to need some help. The results of the auditions hadn't yet been posted.

She told Shorofsky what she'd done; how she'd gone down to Chase School and spoken to Troy, urged him to come and give it a shot on equal terms with the others.

'I want to be a performer more than anything,' she ended, confused at the way her feelings clashed and offered her no simple and clear solutions. 'Am I crazy to give someone else a chance?'

'You're not being crazy,' Shorofsky said, putting down the chalk and turning to face her. 'You're being a *mensch*.'

'A *mensch*? What's that?'

'A person. You're thinking about somebody else, instead of yourself. You know, when you came in here, I thought you were going to try to pump me for the results of the auditions.'

'I never even thought of it.'

'I know. Does that mean you're not interested?' Shorofsky's smile was a study in gentle irony.

'No,' Coco said, drawing imaginary circles on the

desk with her finger, 'I'm interested. But I guess . . . I guess I already know what the result's going to be. Troy's got it.'

'Yes,' Shorofsky persisted, 'but do you know why?'

'Because . . .' Coco hesitated for a moment. 'Because he was the best. On that day, with that song, he was the best.'

'Right. That's what an audition is all about. And that's why I was wrong to cancel the auditions and put Troy forward without giving the others a chance. I was making allowances for other considerations, and Troy deserved better than that. In fact . . .' Shorofsky leaned towards her, lowering his voice to keep his words private as the first of his class members came in through the door. 'In fact, Coco, out of the two of us, you're the one who gave Troy a fair shake. You're growing up, cookie.'

It felt good; even through the disappointment, it felt good. Shorofsky turned back to the board to complete his copying, and Coco made her way down to her usual place as the room filled.

She was remembering a remark of David Reardon's, something that he'd said to them in one of his first sessions when he'd come to the School of the Arts as a newly-qualified teacher with six years of good stage experience behind him. *No matter what kind of an artist you're aspiring to become, first you have to be a human being.* All of the technique and polish in the world is useless if there's nothing inside.

Well, Coco Hernandez, today you made it one step closer. Now it's time to do what Danny would advise.

Look inward. Analyse it. Learn to use it.

9

Orchestra rehearsals for the festival started late; Shorofsky wanted to offer the widest and the richest sound that the School's musical talent could produce, and half of the talent that he'd chosen to use was tied up in mid-term drama presentations.

It meant extra pressure on those players who had to double-up on their spare-time activities while still keeping up their grades and getting their course assignments in on schedule, but Shorofsky wasn't going to feel guilty about that. Life, he always said, very rarely makes allowances - and professional life, never. Most of the dropouts rate at the School of the Arts consisted of kids who just rocked back in terror at the size and the scope of the curriculum. Sometimes it seemed cruel, watching them go out of the doors for the last time and leaving a lot of their dreams behind in the locker room, but the biggest cruelty of all would have been to give them an easy ride.

If Benjamin Shorofsky ever came to doubt this, he could think back to his own experience with Troy Phillips. Shorofsky had been tempted to break the basic rule, and even with the best intentions he'd come close to doing wrong by everyone. It was for this reason that he didn't hesitate to enlist Julie Miller in the festival orchestra's cello section.

Julie's workload was probably higher at this point in the year than it had ever been. Not only was she playing accompaniment for the drama department, but whenever she was able to get a few minutes alone she was working on a piece that she'd chosen to present in competition for the inter-borough musical scholarship. A few minutes alone! It was almost a joke. Most of her rehearsal time so far had been late at night in her one-room apartment, practising her fingering with a rag stuffed under the cello's bridge to deaden the strings. She knew what the Haydn piece looked like, and she knew what the fingering felt like; but so far, she'd only her own imagination to tell her what the extract from the concerto sounded like.

Whichever way you looked at it, she was running hard. There couldn't have been a worse time for her instrument to go missing.

She found out at one of the play rehearsals. She'd left the cello in the instrument storage rack in the music room some five hours before, when she'd been in a rush to catch her geography lesson. After a half-hour break in the Burger King around the corner with Bruno and Danny, she'd hurried back to find an empty space where the case should have been.

Scanning the room, she saw it leaning against a chair over on the opposite side. She stormed over to it, flicking her long blonde hair back in annoyance. She *hated* it when someone touched her cello without permission; it was a phobia that only a musician could ever understand. She unzipped the cover, expecting to find the two hundred year old varnish covered in paw-marks.

But it wasn't her cello.

The cover was hers, but the instrument was one of the school's own practice cellos. It was American-made, no more than five years old. She looked around again, but there was nothing she could do right now; any more thorough search would make her late for the rehearsal, and that would be unpardonable.

She knew that she was playing mechanically, just laying the notes down as written without any infusion of feeling, but she couldn't help it. She was concerned. She'd had the instrument since she was thirteen years old; her mother had taken her to pick it out, letting her choose on intuition alone and keeping its price a secret until it was too late for Julie to go back on her decision. It was more than a fine antique; it was a part of her life, something from the happier times before her parents' divorce.

When the rehearsal was over and all the other instruments were being stowed, Julie took another look around. No question about it, her cello was missing. Under any other circumstances she could have blamed it on a mixup, but the switching of the covers was too deliberate. There was only one explanation. Someone had taken it.

There wasn't the time to make a report - in less than half an hour the janitor would be locking the front doors and switching off all the lights. Besides, that might be hasty – this could still be somebody's mean idea of a joke, although Julie couldn't see any funny side to it. In the morning she'd look again, perhaps get some of the others to help out. If that got her nowhere, then she'd make it official..

'See?' Julie said to Ben Shorofsky when she'd finished the Boccherini passage that had been her tutorial assignment. 'There's no warmth, no depth to the tone. This thing won't speak, period. It's terrible.'

'It's *different*,' Shorofsky conceded.

'How different?'

'Some of the colours are changed slightly. It's softer sounding than yours.'

'The colours haven't changed. They've disappeared.'

'Miller.' Shorofsky allowed himself to get a little stern. He was concerned over Julie's problem – theft in the school was a serious matter, and this was something much more than the disappearance of someone's lunch money – but he couldn't let it blur their academic focus. 'Miller, it was very good. Now play the andante.'

Julie was slightly taken aback. 'Very good? You mean it sounds *better*?'

Enough already! 'Different!' Shorofsky roared, and he pointed to the music. 'Play, Miller!'

'Mister Shorofsky, my cello is two hundred years

old. This is almost brand new. My cello is English, this is American. My . . .'

'I know it's not your cello, Miller. It's an orphan cello. Adopt it. Make it your foster cello. *Play.*'

Julie started to play.

10

After the tutorial lesson, Julie made a formal report. That afternoon, a detective came over from the station house on West Forty-Seventh to get a statement, and Julie was excused the last fifteen minutes of Elizabeth Sherwood's session on American short story writers to go and speak to him. As Sherwood explained the nature of the team research projects that she was handing out, Bruno Martelli was wondering if it would be worth having one of his synthesizers stolen, maybe just a little bitty theft like the pocket-sized Yamaha, in order to get a cast-iron excuse to skip an English lesson. On the whole, probably not - but it was a close-run thing.

Doris Schwartz was picked as a team leader, and she drew her subject out of a bowl. *John O'Hara.*

After the lesson, she went over to Bruno and Leroy.

'Okay, you two,' she said. 'You're drafted.'

Bruno looked at Leroy with a doubt that was only slightly overplayed. 'What do you think?'

Leroy thought it over. 'I think we should wait for a better offer. Somebody who can guarantee us an *A*.'

'Leroy,' Doris said, 'this is the best offer you're going to get. Who else would be willing to carry you?'

'You hear that?' Leroy asked Bruno. 'Carry me?' He turned back to Doris. 'Doris, I am an expert on short stories.'

'Leroy,' Bruno said, '*Weird Comics* does not qualify as short stories.'

The next period was a study hour, so they went up to the library. Danny Amatullo got himself collected along the way to complete the team, and the four of them took over a complete library alcove and stacked the table high with every reference book they could find.

The intention to work was there, but the will somehow wasn't. Within a quarter of an hour, the conversation had turned to the subject of Julie's missing cello.

'I think somebody here, someone in the school, stole the thing.' Doris said, and she started to count off on her fingers. 'He knew where to look, when to go, and what to go for. And who's going to notice another student carrying a cello in a practice case?'

'I think we're supposed to be writing a term paper on John O'Hara,' Leroy said. 'Not who ripped off Julie Miller's cello.'

Bruno looked at him with surprise. 'Don't you care?'

Leroy shrugged. 'Not my business.'

'All right. Suppose it was your instrument that was stolen. What then?'

Leroy slid back his chair and pointed to his feet, which were clad in a gaudy pair of star-spangled trainers over knee-high socks. 'These are my instruments,' he said. 'Anybody tries to mess with them, and they're going to have a whole bunch of trouble to deal with.' And that, apparently, was Leroy's last word on the subject. He returned to the text in front of him, his lips moving slowly as he followed the words. Leroy's reading had improved a lot in the past year, but this was a habit he'd been unable to get rid of.

Doris and Bruno got back to the discussion. 'Where do you go when you want to sell a stolen instrument?' Doris said. 'Do they have used instrument stores?'

'Pawn shop,' Leroy said, without looking up. 'A thief ain't got no time to shop around. He wants to dump what he has, and get. Pawn shop. It's faster.'

'That's a great idea,' Danny said.

'Yeah,' Doris said, with growing enthusiasm. 'All we have to do is check the pawn shops in New York, and I bet we find Julie's cello.' She looked at Danny and Bruno. Both were a little open-mouthed; Leroy, meanwhile, was still trying to ignore the whole conversation. 'I'll take the Bronx,' she suggested.

'That is the dumbest thing I ever heard,' Leroy muttered as Danny brought the Yellow Pages over from the reference shelves. 'You got any idea how many pawn shops there *are* in all of New York?'

They had an answer for the Bronx, soon enough; there were seven. 'I can handle that,' Doris said, but Leroy was still unconvinced.

'Okay,' he said, 'even if we...' He stopped, and

corrected himself. 'Even if *you* find the right pawnshop, how you gonna know it's Julie's cello?'

But Doris wasn't about to be stopped. 'There's a brass plaque on the bottom with her initials on it. I remember.'

'Yeah,' Leroy said, exasperated, 'well I remembered I got something else to do.'

'What?'

'Anything,' Leroy said. He stood up, slammed his book shut, picked up the notes that he'd made, and walked out of the alcove.

Maybe it was some milder form of a deathwish; Leroy's grades hadn't been so hot this term, and even as he'd whipped up the will to do the extra work he found himself being slowly drawn into someone else's problem.

What he really needed was to find some quiet corner where he could study alone. Instead, he took a walk.

A walk's okay, he told himself. A walk's just a way of clearing out your head for the heavy thinking. Doris and the others had been guiding his mind onto a track where he really couldn't afford to let it go. Leroy knew exactly where a check of the Bronx pawnshops would get them; nowhere. They just hadn't thought it through. Somebody stealing a cello wouldn't take it all the way to the Bronx to unload it, not if he wanted to make the trip without some suspicious cop's heavy hand falling on his shoulder; he'd head for somewhere close, but not too close. Somewhere in Manhattan, somewhere uptown.

He headed west, dodging across the wide race-track that was the convergence of Broadway and Seventh. A skateboarder sailed by, a bearded white in his mid-twenties taking a gamble on seeing thirty by riding the traffic; slightly Bohemian and carrying a knapsack, he was hitching rides by grabbing trucks and buses, coasting on around corners, reaching for the next. Nobody paid too much attention; it was probably his regular way of getting around. Once Leroy might have been tempted to try something similar, but not any more. A broken ankle set wrong could end his career before it had even started.

He passed the faded gilt and old marble of the Edison Hotel's rear foyer. Next door was the Lunt Fontanne theatre, where he'd once sneaked in without paying to see a performance of *Peter Pan*. To this day, he'd never told anyone. He'd never found out how the show ended, either, because an assistant manager had found him and thrown him out before the last act began.

At Eighth, he made a turn and started to walk uptown.

I'll make a circle, he thought, pick up a Coke and head around and back. He started to scan the storefronts for a fast food franchise. There was an Orange Julius stall about fifty yards ahead, but before that there was a pawnshop.

In the pawnshop window, there was a cello.

Okay, so that was a cello. Leroy had no cause to think that it was Julie's, so he told himself to keep walking.

His feet didn't listen. With the comradeship of one instrument towards another, they took him into the pawnshop.

The place smelled of fifty years of dust and metal polish. The broker gave him a doubtful look when Leroy told him what he wanted to see, but he went to get the cello from the window. Leroy waited patiently on the customer side of the counter.

'Funny,' the broker said, 'I'd never have picked you for a cello player.'

'I ain't,' Leroy said, turning the cello over to look for the giveaway brass plate. 'I'm a collector.'

'Then you came to the right place. Look at the finish on that thing. Notice...'

But Leroy, having found no plate, was already handing the instrument back across the counter.

'What's this?' the broker said. 'You think you can tell a good cello just by checking the bottom?'

'You got it,' Leroy said, already on his way out of the door.

'Wait!' the broker called after him. 'I got another cello in the back. Betcha it's just what you're looking for. Don't go away.'

Wearily, Leroy let the door close with him still on the inside. This was not welcome news. He watched as the broker re-emerged with yet another instrument, a cello with no cover. 'I took this from a guy on loan,' the broker said as he lifted it onto the counter between them, 'but I've got a hunch the guy ain't never coming back for it.'

Leroy turned it over. There it was, a small metal plate with the initials *JDM* in some fancy scrolled engraving.

This was all he needed.

'You interested?' the broker said.

Leroy turned the cello upright. 'I don't know. What are you asking for it?'

'Oh,' the broker began, switching from *selling* mode to *haggling* mode. 'That's an expensive instrument. Especially *that* one. You see...'

'Let me ask it this way,' Leroy cut in patiently. 'Supposing this cello is stolen, and I can prove it's stolen. And supposing I don't mind telling the cops that this store is handling hot merchandise, since I know -' and here he tapped the counter - '*this cello is definitely stolen. Then* how much do you want for it?'

The broker's friendly expression dropped like a mask. His eyes, sharp as pencil-points, studied Leroy much as one jungle animal might study another of similar size and strength.

The plate with the initials was the problem. If it wasn't for that, he could have thrown Leroy out onto the street; what stopped him was that Leroy had known where to look.

The broker considered it from every angle, including the possibility that two kids might be working in collusion. The goddamned cello might have been in and out of every pawnshop in uptown New York. But could he take that chance?

Leroy waited it out. Facing down the broker didn't bother him at all. Going to the cops, now, *that* would be something to sweat about; Leroy and New York's Finest were like the sodium and water that had exploded on contact in last week's chemistry class. He could have gone back and told Julie, and Julie could have phoned her detective, and maybe sometime tomorrow they'd get around to sending someone over to take a look ... by which time the broker would have put two and two together, and the cello would be off the premises.

No, this kind of pressure didn't bother Leroy at all.

It sure was bothering the broker, though.

11

The cop was six feet four and pot-bellied, but even so his uniform looked as if it had been handed down to him by an older brother who had quit the force ten years before. He spent a good five seconds contemplating the lanky black teenager who had just passed him going in the opposite direction wearing drum-majorette shoes and carrying a cello, and then he called out, 'Hey, kid!'

Leroy paused, and then turned to look back. 'Me?'

The cop nodded. 'Where you going with the big fiddle?'

Leroy looked down at the cello, thinking, and then with his most winning smile he looked back to the cop. 'I'm on my way to my cello lesson,' he said.

The cop walked over, and stood facing Leroy. 'Son,' he said, 'I'll tell you what. You play me a song on that thing, and I'll apologise for having any doubts as to how you came by it. Okay?'

Leroy's smile wavered for an instant, but he wasn't one to throw in the towel so easily. 'Okay,' he said. 'What do you want to hear?'

'Oh,' the cop said, 'I don't know. How about *Flow Gently, Sweet Afton*?'

'I don't know it.'

'Danny Boy.'

Leroy started to shake his head, but the cop was quick.

'Happy Birthday.'

The cop rocked confidently back and forth on his crepe soles as Leroy began looking around, apparently searching for something. Like a back door that would offer him a fast exit from the street.

'Lose something?' the cop said.

'Music chair,' Leroy explained. 'You can't play these things standing up. You have to sit.'

The cop pointed to the nearest fire hydrant. 'How about that?' he said. 'Looks about the right height.'

Leroy walked over to the fire hydrant, and wouldn't you know it, the damned thing *was* the right height. He took the bow in his right hand, assumed the position, and stroked a string. Wrong pitch. He tightened up a little, tried again. Leroy had now reached the limit of his practical orchestral knowledge. Why couldn't Julie Miller have played the harmonica? Leroy could just about limp his way through *Orange Blossom Special* on the harmonica.

The cop was waiting. From Leroy's position he looked more like ten feet tall than six.

'Well?' the cop said.

Leroy looked up, in innocence. 'You're not talking about the white *Happy Birthday*, are you?'

There had been a time when Leroy had been no stranger to the back seat of a NYPD blue-and-white. Five minutes later, he was given the chance to get re-acquainted.

12

'It was all a mistake,' Doris Schwartz insisted. 'A dumb mistake.'

The detectives' Squad Room in the precinct house was a featureless office with a view of some rusty air ducts less than six feet out from the window. The room itself seemed to be a kind of meeting point for all of the building's plumbing systems; painted pipes ran down each corner and across the ceiling. Every few seconds, a glugging would come from a different part of the room. It was like sitting in a giant's stomach and listening to the after-effects of an underdone pizza.

Leroy had been allowed one phonecall, and a scratch team had been sent out for his rescue. Doris and Coco Hernandez sat across a desk from a detective called Harmon, whose eyes were as expressive as a couple of chips of slate. Leroy was out of it, sitting at the end of the desk and looking steamed. He'd used up all of his resources of persuasion, and they'd got him exactly nowhere.

'You see,' Doris went on, 'we were in the library trying to figure who took the cello.' She glanced at Julie for support, but Julie was out of it for the moment. She was sitting some way apart, examining the instrument minutely for marks or scratches. A mother who'd grabbed her only child out of the hands of a would-be molester could hardly have shown a deeper concern.

'Danny came up with this idea,' Coco explained, but Doris interrupted.

'I think it was really Bruno who came up with it,' Doris said.

'Oh,' Coco said, and she smiled and shrugged at Detective Harmon. Harmon sighed heavily, and his eyes seemed to chase an invisible butterfly up and out of sight. 'I wasn't there.'

'It was me,' Leroy said miserably, and they all looked at him. 'I was the stupid jerk who thought of checking the pawnshops. I'm getting what I deserve.'

Julie had checked the pitch on each of the cello's strings; now she began to play.

It was one of the slower passages from the Haydn concerto. There was no piano handy to complement her, but the cello line stood up pretty well on its own. All activity in the Squad Room had stopped; a pick-pocket who had been in the middle of giving his statement to a sergeant on the next desk sat with his mouth hanging open.

Julie smiled. This was more like it. It was something to get a decent hearing of the Haydn for the first time, as well.

As she finished, Dectective Harmon cleared his throat.

'If that ain't your cello,' he said, 'it sure as hell

ought to be.' He turned to Leroy. 'Get out of here.'

Doris looked at Coco, and they both grinned.

There was just a pop of imploding air to denote where Leroy had been sitting only a moment before.

The cancellation of Norman Benzer's oboe tutorial had given Shorofsky a gap in his timetable; Norman's mother had telephoned in to say that he had the 'flu, and it hardly seemed fair to insist that he should come in and play when he could barely breathe. Purple-faced woodwind players weren't in the greatest demand on the orchestra circuits, unless you included the Muppets in the survey.

The break was unexpected, but it was welcome. It gave Shorofsky a chance to catch up on his administrative paperwork, something that he'd allowed to slip by in the constant bustle of the last few days. Top of the heap in his neglected desk drawer were the forms for the Festival of the Musical Arts. Now that the lineup and the lead had finally been decided, he could get the papers in and beat the deadline by a good three weeks.

It was something of a relief, the way things had worked out. Troy was now attending the School of the Arts on three days out of every week, and his other educational needs were being covered at Chase. His first two weeks in class had still been a little uneasy, but the wall had come down brick by brick as the other students had realised that they were doing themselves no favours by making allowances for Troy. Natural ability had already put him a little way ahead, and they were just fixing to increase his lead.

No, the Festival and the run-up to it were going to be good for everybody: he'd already noticed one or two changes in Coco Hernandez; she'd been on top of the hill for so long that she'd been starting to regard it as a right, not something that she'd have to work to maintain. Knocks to the ego were never pleasant to see, but sometimes they were necessary. In any case, Coco seemed to be handling it well. The way that she'd come through the death of her *abuelita*, the grandmother to whom she'd been so close, had been evidence enough of that.

Bruno Martelli had been another worry; Shorofsky had begun to sense that there were difficulties, not in the work that he was turning in but rather somewhere behind it. Problems at home weren't uncommon at the School of the Arts - parents often couldn't understand the workload and the attitudes of mind that the school encouraged - but none of the usual reasons seemed likely to apply in Bruno's case. Shorofsky had met Angelo Martelli on more than one occasion, and he'd been impressed by the man's enthusiasm for what his son was doing. Bruno had several thousand dollars' worth of electronic equipment, all financed on a cabdriver's pay; Angelo carried cassettes of all his son's work and made a point of playing them to his customers.

Shorofsky smiled to himself as he rummaged through the drawer. Perhaps Angelo ought to take out some special insurance. Exposure to Bruno's style of music could come as a pretty nasty surprise to anyone who'd been raised on an exclusive diet of the classics. Something deep inside Shorofsky still twinged with pain when he remembered *Edvard Münch; A Howling in the Void.*

No, any troubles that Bruno was having wouldn't be because he was meeting resistance at home. Shorofsky had been wondering whether to take him aside and fish around a little to see if he could help, but then he'd noticed something that reassured him. There had been a slight change in Bruno's approach to composition; nothing too significant, just a shift in mood that told Shorofsky that the boy was finding his own way around his difficulties. As always, art and humanity were strengthening each other.

Two more layers down, Shorofsky found something that snapped his mind away from his responsibilities of supervision for a moment. It was the tutor's endorsement form for Julie Miller's scholarship entry. She'd given it to him - what? Almost six weeks ago? And it had been shuffled in with the festival papers. He turned it over, scanned down the notes on the reverse side.

Three days! It was only three days from the deadline! Putting all of the other papers to one side, Shorofsky took a Bic from his jacket pocket and spread the form on the blotter before him.

To miss the date would have been unforgivable. Without his endorsement, Julie's entry would have been disallowed. He spent so much time turning down excuses for the non-appearance of work that there was no way that he could go easy on himself for this one. Skin of your teeth, Benjamin. You deserve to sweat a little.

It would be a mistake to suppose that Julie didn't actually need the scholarship, just because she had all the appearance of a wealthy WASP background; white anglo-saxon protestants had their problems, too. Julie Miller's included her parents' wrecked marriage and a mother who took pride in the image of her daughter as a fine, sensitive cellist but who couldn't quite grasp the need for rigorous application that underpinned the image. Her father had moved out of town - Detroit, or somewhere further into the Midwest - and the costs of running two homes on a single executive salary meant that times had become as tight for Julie as they were for anybody.

Shorofsky got the form completed. He decided that he'd better make it a priority, and get it down to the school office and into the mail before he did anything else.

Mrs Berg was in charge at the office, as always. Shorofsky's request was a simple one - to get an envelope typed and stamped so that Julie's form could go in the afternoon's mail - but with Mrs Berg, nothing was ever quite straightforward. Danny Amatullo had once been overheard by Lydia Grant saying that Mrs Berg was a nice, *nice* lady blessed with a room-temperature IQ. Not too kind, but not too inaccurate, either.

Shorofsky was relieved to see that the form was passed to one of the other clerks to be dealt with... but Mrs Berg wasn't going to let him go so easily. Her reason for handing the work along was that she wanted to persuade Shorofsky to buy one of a sheaf of charity football cards that she'd brought in.

'You see,' she explained, 'if the Rams win by four points, then that means they will cover this three and a half point spread. But if they only win by a field goal...'

'Are you sure this is a legal thing?' Shorofsky interrupted. He wouldn't have known a field goal if one had felled him.

'Oh, my,' Mrs Berg said breathily, 'yes, the man who gave them to me said all the money you lose goes to this charity he runs.'

'And you believe him?'

'Oh, my, yes. You see, he also said you don't have to declare any money you might win. It's tax free because it comes from a charity, you see. He explained the whole thing to me.'

'Couldn't I just donate and get a receipt? That's the way most charities work.' A door opened behind Shorofsky, and Elizabeth Sherwood came into the office. He nodded amiably to her as she went by, but the smile that he got in return seemed more than a little strained.

'That's the way most of them work,' Mrs Berg went on as Elizabeth stopped by the mailboxes to check if there was anything for her, 'but he said this works differently.'

Shorofsky nodded. He didn't understand, but what the hell. It was only a dollar, even if the whole deal was probably as crooked as the slalom run in a skateboard park. He took out his Bic again, and started to fill out some of the choices on the card as Elizabeth joined him at the desk.

'Mrs Berg,' she said, 'if you have a second . . . could you check my file and see how much sick leave I'm entitled to?'

'Right away,' Mrs Berg said, and she moved away to the filing area.

Without looking up, Shorofsky said, 'Coming down with something?'

'I'm not sure,' Elizabeth said.

'There's a lot of that going around.'

There was a moment's silence, as if Elizabeth was regretting the transparent evasion and was trying to think of a way of showing it whilst still keeping the truth to herself. Then she said, 'Mister Shorofsky . . . do you ever get just plain fed up? Do you ever start to feel like you're beating your head against a stone wall?'

Shorofsky thought it over. 'No,' he said. 'I've never known a day here that hasn't come up with at least one surprise and at least one thing to give me satisfaction.'

'You never had the feeling that you're doing the same thing over and over? You never want to do something far out and crazy . . . just to do it?'

Shorofsky slid one of the football cards over to

her. 'Try filling out one of these,' he said. 'Far out, I'm not sure about, but crazy certainly applies.'

He smiled a farewell and then turned to go out into the lobby, leaving his card and his dollar on the desk behind him. At that moment, Mrs Berg arrived with Elizabeth's file.

'Ten days,' she announced. 'It says here that you have ten days' sick leave entitlement left.'

Elizabeth nodded thoughtfully, and started away from the counter. After a couple of steps, she came back and reached for one of the football cards.

'I'll get this to you tomorrow,' she told Mrs Berg. 'I've always been a sucker for a worthy cause.'

When David Reardon had passed the selection board to fill the vacant post of drama teacher at the School of the Arts, nobody had been more relieved than his father. When Reardon had first made the decision that he wanted to be a professional actor, he'd been around the same age as most of the kids that he now taught; his father had put a brave face on and made the best of it, saying that at least he now knew what kind of work his son was going to be out of.

But apart from a couple of really lean patches when he'd had to clear tables and wash dishes in the Flame Steaks restaurant on West Forty-Eighth and Broadway, Reardon had been able to keep up a decent employment record in a business where such an achievement tended to be exceptional. He'd always appeared young for his age, which meant that even up until he was twenty-three he was taking teenage parts with no loss of conviction but with a big reduction in headaches for theatre managements over state laws on the employment of juveniles. Afterwards, he just kept on working; he'd made his mark, and there were quite a number of casting directors who knew him and liked his work.

So teaching, for Dave Reardon, wasn't the refuge of a professional failure. He'd first been led around to the idea by a girlfriend that he'd been trying to impress at the time; she helped out with a youth theatre over on the West Side of Manhattan, and he'd shown a willingness to go along. He and the girl had gone their separate ways, but the bug had stayed with him. Teaching drama wasn't an alternative to acting; it was all of the same satisfactions, plus an indefinable something extra.

The school itself and the people in it were also an endless source of interest and curiosity. You never knew what was going to be asked of you next – especially when it was someone like Mrs Berg doing the asking.

'Mr Reardon,' she said, catching him up in the corridor one day. 'Do you know much about sports and things?'

'Uh ... a little,' Reardon said, wondering exactly what might be on the papers that Mrs Berg was studying with such puzzlement.

'Well, then,' she said, 'Maybe you can help me.'

There didn't seem to be any escape. Reardon

stopped, and waited to hear it.

'You see, I forget,' Mrs Berg said, shuffling the papers and checking both sides as if she was looking for a ladybug that had somehow got mixed up in there. 'Is it the Raiders or the Chargers who never do diddley on artificial turf?'

Leroy had to walk around Danny Amatullo and Diana Huddleston to get into the English class. They were smack in the middle of the corridor, and there sure as hell wasn't any way to get *between* them.

He almost sighed. White folks looked so dumb when they fell for this whole love thing; a little surge of the hormones and they turned into Nelson Eddy and Jeanette MacDonald. Only three weeks ago, they'd had the knives out for each other - Diana because Danny had been feeding her bought-in dialogue, and Danny because Diana was swallowing it without a complaint. Now look at them.

Give it another three weeks, Leroy thought, and they'll be back to nodding *Hi* in the corridors as they pass.

Leroy had other things to think about, as well. His contribution to the team effort of the John O'Hara term paper was progressing exactly nowhere.

He supposed that there were ways around it, but he already knew that none of the obvious ones were going to get him anywhere. Doris Schwartz had already joked that the team was probably going to carry him, and there was no way that Leroy was about to let that happen. Cheating might get him through, but in the end the only one that he'd really be cheating would be himself.

No, Sherwood was always going on about how, if there was any problem or anything they wanted to ask, her door was always open. Well, now she was going to get a guest on the invitation. It had taken Leroy a lot of soul-searching to get this far; showing enough interest in school work to actually go to a teacher and ask questions - one-to-one, with nobody pushing him and nobody telling him what to do - tended to go against everything that Leroy in his earlier life had believed.

But that had been in his earlier life. That was before he'd discovered dancing, real, disciplined hard-work dancing as opposed to just freaking around to a boom-box in a back alley to impress the girls. Study was the price for going on... but for Leroy and dancing, no price could be too high.

He walked into the classroom. Sherwood wasn't there.

A substitute teacher was seated at the desk, glancing over her lesson plan. She looked up as Leroy came in, the first of the students to arrive.

'Good morning,' she said. 'I'm Miss Hardy.'

'Where's Sherwood?'

'I imagine she's sick.'

'What with?'

'They don't tell me that. They just tell me a teacher will be absent and then they tell me where to go.'

The bell rang, and the classroom filled. Leroy sat in silence as the roll was called, feeling as if he'd been robbed. It had taken a week to get himself up to this, and now the enemy had run off and gone to ground. He couldn't talk to no *substitute*. It had to be Sherwood or nobody.

13

After more than a week of English from the substitute teacher, Leroy was starting to get distinctly uneasy. Miss Hardy was fine as far as the broad details went, but at best Leroy felt that he was marking time. He'd got his sights fixed on making Sherwood hold good on her offer, and nothing less was going to do.

He tried, but nothing seemed to work. Leroy had the feeling that this O'Hara guy was getting at something, and if only he could have a push in the right direction the day might break and he'd suddenly understand what it was. A couple of times he'd hung around at the end of the lesson, but when Miss Hardy had seen him waiting at the back of the room she'd hurriedly gathered her papers together and rushed out. That had made him spend some time in front of one of the makeup room mirrors, looking at himself from every angle and wondering what it was about him that made some white folks take on so. After all, he didn't even carry a knife to school these days - not unless you counted the spring-loaded flicker that he kept hooked on the inside of his jacket or the long stiletto in his locker.

It would have been easy just to give in and let

Doris and the others carry his load. They probably wouldn't even notice that they were doing it. But that wasn't the idea.

In the end, he went down to the school office to speak to Mrs Berg. His idea was to come up with some reason why he had to know Sherwood's home address. The truth would have been the best reason of all, but somehow the truth didn't sound right.

As it happened, he needn't have worried. Before he had a chance to concoct an excuse, Mrs Berg had given him the address that he needed, and something more.

The apartment block wasn't exactly Park Avenue, but it was better than he'd expected. The foyer was carpeted, and there was one of those canvas awnings with a frilled edge that stretched about five yards out over the pavement and gave the tenants somewhere to stand while they watched all the off-duty cabs going by whenever it rained. Sherwood lived up on the fifth floor.

Leroy knocked on the door, and waited. There was one of those little beady glass eye things in the centre panel; standing before it made him uncomfortable, but he didn't have any choice. After a few moments, he heard a couple of locks being disengaged.

The door opened as far as the security chain would allow, and Elizabeth Sherwood looked out. She seemed wary, as if she couldn't really believe that it was Leroy Johnson standing there.

'Leroy?' she said uncertainly.

Leroy looked her over. She had that drawn-out, spaniel-eyed look that women got whenever they'd been crying. In fact, Sherwood looked as if she'd spent the whole of the last eight days on a crying jag; she even looked a few pounds lighter for it, and the loss wasn't an improvement.

'I brought you something from school,' Leroy said.

She hesitated for a moment, and then freed the security chain to let him in.

Leroy stepped into the apartment. It looked neat – too neat, as if someone had been obsessively tidying it, over and over. He looked at Sherwood and said, 'You been sick?'

'No,' she said, closing the door behind him.

'Then what's wrong?'

'Who said anything was wrong?'

'You.'

'When did I say that?'

'Just now when I asked if you been sick, and you didn't get on me about bad grammar.'

That got him a weak smile, at least. It looked like the first one for some time.

'What's wrong,' she said, 'is that I think I broke something.' She moved across to the window and looked out at the skyline without really seeing it. 'My ex-husband died last week,' she said.

Leroy was at a loss. 'I thought... you said you broke something.'

'I did. I even saw it coming... I thought I was used to it. All the excitement when there's a production coming up. All the chatter about costumes and music and sets. All the groans and gripes when I hand out homework assignments...' She smiled and looked at the floor, but it was more a smile of bitterness than anything else. After a moment the bitterness won, and the smile died. 'What I teach has value, damn it, and I'm sick and tired of apologising for what I do. I am sick and tired of begging people to listen to me... sick and tired of having to coax people to speak the language without sounding like they only started to learn it yesterday. And then when the wire came about Nick's death, no-one on his side of the family had even had the decency to tell me that he'd been ill. It was like I didn't matter. To him, to the school, to anyone anywhere on this damn planet. That's when something inside broke.'

She turned and sat, suddenly and heavily, on the couch. Leroy took a couple of steps closer, but he didn't sit beside her.

'You matter to me,' he said, and she smiled. He could see straight away that he hadn't got through; she was taking it as just one of those meaningless things you say to someone that's having a bad time. The smile was about as accurate a register of her feelings as the out-of-date sales total on a McDonald's storefront. He sat himself down across from her, and searched for the words.

'I don't mean to be puttin' down what's hurting you,' he said, 'but you've really got a bad case of white folk's blues.' That got her hooked; she didn't know what the hell he was talking about. 'You see,' he explained, 'black folks know what the blues are all about, you know? They know it's just a part of the whole deal. But white folks . . . well, it seems to me a lot of times they get scared when the blues come by and they don't get into it. It's like they save it all up for one big bad time. Like what you're going through now.'

'You said it,' she agreed, and Leroy could see that he'd given her something to hold on to.

'Ain't nobody gets it all,' he pressed on. 'You ever seen Bruno Martelli try to act? You can't be perfect and happy all the time.'

'And you can't conjugate verbs worth spit.'

'Not on my own, I can't.'

She got up, and went over to the door. She opened it wide and said, but not in an unfriendly way, 'Get out of here. I'm going to cry again.' And then, to allay his concern: 'A good kind of crying. Doesn't scare me at all.'

He watched her for a moment, just to be sure. Then he said, 'You got it,' and bounced off the couch.

But before he'd gone two steps outside, she called him back.

'Hey,' she said. 'I thought you brought me something from school.'

Leroy braked and turned. He'd almost forgotten. He dug in his pocket, and came out with a crumpled envelope. He tossed it to her, and she caught it.

'Packers, Jets, and the Rams,' he explained as she tore it open. 'Mrs Berg asked me to give it to you. All beat the spread, more than thirty bucks. Congratulations.'

He flipped her a goodbye wave and left her standing there, counting the money in the doorway and giggling helplessly.

He didn't have what he'd originally set out for, but that could wait. Until she started taking her classes again, sometime tomorrow.

14

The finals for the inter-borough musical scholarship awards were held in a rented hall on Lexington, almost in the shadow of the Chrysler building. It was hardly an ideal venue; every ten minutes or so the auditorium shook with a subliminal rumble as the Times Square shuttle ran underneath. The lighting wasn't so hot and the audience seats felt like some kind of punishment, but still there was a near-capacity turnout. Every hopeful music student had brought along a supporting entourage of friends, relatives, sponsors and well-wishers; the atmosphere was good, its edge keen, and standards were high.

Julie Miller's backup was as good as anybody's, with the exception of fifteen year-old Martin Gish who played a solo piece two places ahead of Julie. Gish had brought along with him a whole dynasty of Gishes, enough of them to fill three rows of the auditorium. He was obviously the pride of a large family where things to be proud of were almost as scarce as money. Martin Gish played with a fierce intensity, screening out everything around him and showing none of the nervousness that had been evident as he'd stumbled onto the stage.

Julie went on second to last. She knew that, unless the final competitor turned in something really special, it was going to be between her and the boy. Everyone else had shown serious flaws – hesitancy, lack of familiarity with the notes as written, a couple of examples of sloppy fingering. Julie had no worries on the technical side, but she'd have to match the energy of Martin Gish's attack.

When her turn came around, she and Bruno walked out onto the stage. The hall might be lousy, but the charge in the air was immense. As Bruno was taking his seat at the piano, Julie glanced out into the audience. Her people were there, Shorofsky, Doris and Danny; Coco Hernandez was just sliding in from the end of the row, her hair whipped by the wind and her breathing hard as if she'd run all the way from West Forty-Sixth.

Julie played well. The Haydn piece sang.

But when the head of the judges stood up to announce the results, Martin Gish had got it.

Three rows of Gishes went wild. Martin Gish smiled and glanced around in embarrassment, just another fifteen year old kid now that the cello was out of his hands. Julie took a deep breath, and looked at the ground.

It wasn't unfair. Gish had been good. But she'd wanted to win.

'Thank you all for coming,' the judge was saying, 'you should *all* be proud,' but the words were of little comfort. Second place was no good to anybody; no scholarship, no recognition, none of the essential feedback of success that Julie had come to need to sustain her as a performer.

She looked up; everybody was out of their seats, and Shorofsky and the others were gathering around her. She tried to fake a smile. It was an awkward moment; whatever was said first had a ninety per cent chance of coming out wrong.

Such odds weren't likely to discourage Danny Amatullo; after all, he'd made a life's work out of putting his foot in his mouth. 'Hey, don't worry about it, kid,' he said. 'It's only your career.'

'Mister Amatullo,' Shorofsky began heavily, but Danny threw up his hands in self-defence.

'Only kidding,' he protested.

Bruno said, 'Well, think of the great liner notes.'

Shorofsky turned to him in puzzlement. 'Liner notes?'

'You know, the stuff they always write on the backs of albums about what a tough life the artist had.' He went on earnestly to Julie, 'Believe me, early success makes lousy liner notes. That's why I'm holding back.'

Julie started to laugh, the ice broken, and Doris pitched in.

'Oh, I got lots of liner notes,' she said. 'I remember once, I tried out for the lead in this musical. I thought I had it for sure.' She shook her head. 'Forget it. I didn't even make it past the first cut. I was devastated. I didn't eat for hours. Hours!'

Bruno checked his watch; it was almost three-thirty in the afternoon. Lydia Grant would be expecting them for a dance rehearsal at four. As Bruno went to get his score and the others gathered their books together, Coco asked, 'Which musical?'

'*The Sound of Music.*'

'The lead in *The Sound of Music*? The Julie Andrews part?'

'Yeah, well … the director said I looked too Hare Krishna for the part.'

They had to go. They knew that they could only try to raise Julie's spirits up to a certain level beyond which the jokiness would become embarrassing. Julie was going to have to cover the rest of the distance on her own.

The hall was almost empty as she went to zip her cello back into its case. She held it for a moment getting the same kind of comfort as she might from an old rag doll, and then she stowed it and closed the lid.

Up on the stage, two janitors in stained old coveralls were rolling the piano away. Shorofsky was still there, waiting for her. She tried to smile, to show that everything was okay.

'And behind the smile?' Shorofsky said.

'I'm fine, really.'

They started to walk up the aisle towards the exits. Shorofsky said, 'If you're fine after losing a competition, there's something wrong with you. And if there is something wrong with you, then you are not fine. So, what?'

Julie shrugged as they came out into the foyer. Only a couple of people were still hanging around.

he departure of Martin Gish and his relatives had half-emptied the building within a minute.

She said, 'More practice time. That's all I need, more practice time.'

'You practised very hard. I heard you.'

Shorofsky opened one of the main doors to let Julie and her cello through. Outside on Lexington, he later afternoon traffic was building up.

'Obviously not hard enough,' Julie said. She said it quietly, because she wasn't sure that she wanted Shorofsky to hear.

15

The next day, Elizabeth Sherwood was back in school. She picked up the threads of her disrupted schedule, thanked everybody who asked after her health, and on passing Leroy Johnson in the corridor she gave him a wink that was so fast and so unexpected that he was still wondering an hour later whether or not it had happened.

Ben Shorofsky continued to marvel at the way in which Troy Phillips was progressing. He was taking voice classes and his grasp of theory, though a little slow, was getting better.

'Well, Troy,' he said at the end of their weekly tutorial, 'how's everything going?'

'I thought you were supposed to tell me that,' Troy said.

'What I meant was...'

'I know,' Troy said quickly. 'It was a joke. Everything's fine, thanks, Mister Shorofsky. My teachers back at Chase say they've noticed an improvement in the work I'm doing there, as well. I can't really explain it - I just feel better about everything.'

Thank God for music, Shorofsky thought to himself as he walked down the practice room corridor after the session. Opener of minds as well as hearts. The satisfied glow that the thought gave him died a little as he heard the muffled strains of a familiar cello line coming from behind one of the doors of the practice cubicles.

A delicate enough piece, it was being murdered. It was like a lullaby being thrashed out with all the passion of *The Ride of the Valkyries*. It was like an adagio played with hammers on a kettledrum.

It was Julie Miller's scholarship piece.

Shorofsky listened for a while, and then knocked and entered.

Julie looked up as he came in. She'd been getting a little overheated, playing the same intricate sequence of bars over and over and getting less satisfied with every attempt.

'Miller,' Shorofsky said, 'why are you torturing the passage? We both know you can do it, you proved that yesterday. It was perfect, absolutely perfect.'

'Thanks, but if it was so perfect, why didn't I win?'

Shorofsky closed the door behind him. 'Because perfect is impossible,' he said.

'But you just said...'

'I was talking about technical perfection; flawless bowing, flawless fingering, a flawless rendition of every note on the stave. That's possible, and that's what you delivered. But *musical* perfection... never.' Julie was looking confused, so Shorofsky went on, 'Tell me, do you think Casals was the greatest cellist in the world? Or Rubenstein the greatest pianist? Or Galway on the flute?'

'Who knows?' Julie said. They were questions without answers.

'Exactly! Certainly they all possess tremendous technique, but is this why hundreds line up in the rain to buy tickets? To hear technique? No and absolutely not. They line up to hear these people make music. Am I making any sense at all?'

'I think so,' Julie said, but it was a struggle. Ever since she'd started with the instrument, her entire focus had been on technique; it had had to be, because she'd only been starting out on the long road of practice and polish that would make technique a second nature that would live in her fingers without taking up all of the concentration space in her mind.

Shorofsky pulled over one of the music chairs, and sat down beside her.

'Listen to me,' he said, and his expression was so serious that it was almost grave. 'During the war, technique was my survival. Each day I would practice, for hours. It was my "great escape" from all the pain around me. But it was only after the war that I could put all of my feelings into the notes. Only then did I play music, real music.' He hitched the chair a little closer. 'It was the feelings that changed the technique; changed it into music. It's what you're going to have to do. Miller, there will be other competitions. That's why I'm telling you all this. Because, win or lose, you must take the joy and the disappointment and put them here.' He leaned across, and patted the strings; they hummed a little, momentarily stirred into life. 'Put Julie in here, and they'll line up for blocks.'

'Even in the rain?'

'Even in the rain.'

'I'll try,' Julie began, but it seemed that she was going to have to save her efforts for a little later. The practice room door burst open, and Doris Schwartz came bowling in.

She stood before them for a few moments, gasping for air. She looked as if she'd sprinted a circuit of the entire school to find Julie, and now that she'd found her she didn't have the breath to deliver the message.

'Julie,' she managed at last. 'Hurry up, your dad's on the office phone.'

'Who?' Julie said, disbelieving.

'Your dad,' Doris repeated. 'Now, come on.'

For a long moment, Julie didn't move. Not a muscle. Doris did her best to jerk her out of it.

'Julie,' she explained with over-extended patience, 'the cord won't reach. We've got to go to the phone.'

Julie made a half-move to get up, as if she was waking out of a dream.

'Miller,' Shorofsky siad, 'trust me. I'll guard the cello. *Go.*'

Somebody must have misheard. She hadn't spoken to her dad in months, maybe as much as a year. The call was for someone else. perhaps even some other Julie Miller.

But she went.

★

The *hold* light on the office phone was still flashing when Julie and Doris got there; whoever it was on the other end of the line, he hadn't gone away. Julie picked up the receiver.

'Hello?' she said tentatively.

'Peanut? Is that you?'

There was no mistake. 'Hi, daddy,' she said, doing her best to sound as if she wasn't nervous.

'You got a date for lunch on Wednesday?'

'Lunch?' What was he talking about? 'Uh... no. Are you coming to New York?'

'I'll be there about ten-thirty. How about if I pick you up at twelve o'clock? We'll go someplace nice. That sound okay?'

Someplace nice. That probably meant fresh linen on the tables, every table in its own alcove made private with flowers and potted palms, every alcove angled towards a big picture window with a view of the Manhattan skyline through tinted glass. There'd be lobster on the menu, and the music would be live. An awfully long way from a Popeye's Fried Chicken.

'Sure,' she said, feeling anything but. 'Are you on business, or...' She let it hang.

'Very important business. I've got something I want to tell you.'

'Like what?'

'Hey, that's unfair. I want to tell you in person. It's that kind of news.' He waited to see if there would be any more reaction, but there was none. 'Wednesday, at twelve o'clock?'

'Twelve o'clock.'

''Bye, Peanut.'

''Bye.' Julie cradled the phone. It had been impossible to tell what he had in mind, and now she was going to have to wait to hear. Almost a year with just the occasional dashed-off letter to keep in touch, and on her birthday an expensive present brought by messenger service and probably picked out by his secretary; now she was supposed to sit and be torn up by anticipation until he landed at JFK. Oh, daddy, understanding the other person's point of view was never one of your strong points.

Anticipation wouldn't describe what she was feeling. Dread might come a little closer to it.

Doris Schwartz had plenty that she ought to be doing, but she couldn't tear herself away from the practice room door. Julie had dived out of the school office as if she'd forgotten that Doris was there.

Shorofsky had gone by the time that she got back to the practice room, but he'd stayed true to his word and brought in a passing freshman student to watch the cello. The boy, a little Hispanic who'd shown an exceptional talent for the flute, was staring at the instrument as if expecting it to speak.

Now, Doris listened to Julie attacking the same passage, over and over. No more than four bars would go by without some mistake, and then she'd go back to the beginning and try again. Every time, the attempt got shorter. Finally Doris was startled to hear a distinct thump as the music book hit the door only inches from her ear.

She knocked, but didn't go in.

There was a gap of a few moments, and then the door opened and Julie looked out. She didn't appear to have been crying, but her eyes were bright with suppressed frustration. She stepped back to let Doris enter.

'Julie,' Doris said with real concern, 'is everything all right?'

Julie picked up the book, which was lying face-down behind the door with some of its pages creased up underneath. 'Oh, hi, Doris,' she said with a breeziness that was obviously forced. 'I just... knocked my book over by accident.'

Some accident, and they both knew it. There was an awkward kind of silence, and then Doris said, '*Nu*?'

'No,' Julie said, misunderstanding. 'Actually, it's an old book.'

'Not the book. *Nu*. It's a yiddish word. It means "well"?'

'Oh. Well, what?'

'Well, good news or bad news?'

Julie's smile was strained. 'No jokes, Doris, please.'

'It's not a joke, it's a question. Your father, the phone call, was it good news or bad news?'

'Oh, that,' Julie said, suddenly evasive. 'That was nothing.'

Doris wasn't about to let go. 'That was nothing? From the look on your face when you hung up, I thought he reversed the charges.' She paused, and then; 'Or worse?'

Julie hovered for a moment, but she could see that Doris was determined to follow this one right down to the ground.

'It was that easy to see?' she said.

'Yeah, it was that easy to see. Now, come on. These ears are hungry for details.'

'Really, there's ... nothing to tell.'

Doris watched her for a long moment, and decided that so much was enough. If Julie wasn't prepared to meet her halfway ... she started towards the door.

'I'm just scared,' Julie said suddenly, and Doris turned back.

'Of what?'

'He said he had something important to tell me.'

'And you just automatically assumed that it's bad news. You know, you really ...'

'The last time he said he had something important to tell me,' Julie interrupted, 'it was that he and mom were getting divorced.'

'Ah.' With a precedent like that, it would be hard not to get apprehensive. Doris said, 'But listen, maybe it's good news. Maybe they're getting back together.'

'Back together?' In its own modest way, the idea was something of a bombshell. It simply hadn't occurred to Julie. But the more she tried it on, the better she liked it.

‘Yeah,’ Doris pressed on, ‘a reconciliation. That’s what my folks did. They were split for a while, and then they worked it out and got back together.’

‘I never thought of a reconciliation.’

‘Well,’ Doris said, moving to leave, ‘think about it now.’

‘I will,’ Julie said. ‘Thanks.’

‘Don’t mention it. Ciao.’

‘Ciao.’

A reconciliation. Oh, wow. Oh, please.

Julie lifted the cello, took her bow in hand, and started to play. Her technique was perfect. The music flowed.

16

Coco knew that there wasn't any show rehearsal scheduled for that morning, but there was somebody at the auditorium piano down in the orchestra pit. Standing at the top of the aisle in the empty theatre, she found it a little spooky; all those empty seats, the bare, unlit stage with just a couple of lunchroom chairs and then a long stretch of nothing all the way back to the paint bridge and the brick scene-dock wall, the lonely sound of the echoing piano that seemed to come from everywhere and nowhere.

It was spooky, but not in the sense of being scary; it was the odd, after-hours feeling of a place that you've come to love when there's just you and the atmosphere and no-one else to share. Coco leaned on the back row of the seating, and listened for a while.

There was no mistaking the hands on the piano; nobody else in the school played quite like Bruno Martelli. Those hands were going to get him a lot of recognition some day, whatever he felt about his liner notes.

And yet, there was something different about the music that he was making. Hard to put a finger on it, but the Bruno playing down there sounded about ten years older, ten years wiser. Coco hesitated for a while, but then she slowly descended and climbed to sit on the edge of the pit.

He looked up at her from a pool of warmth made by the light over the music stand. He let the melody end on its own, not forcing it. 'Hi, Coco,' he said.

'Hi, Bruno. New song?'

'Something I've been working on.'

'Something special?'

'Yeah, I suppose it is. Taking me a long time to get it just right.' He picked out the melody line once more, slowly and using only one finger, stripping the song down to its barest essentials.

Then he looked up at Coco again.

'It's for my dad,' he explained.

17

The restaurant for lunch on Wednesday wasn't exactly as Julie had imagined it, but she hadn't been far wrong. Whereas a couple of years ago she'd have blended in without a second thought, now she felt awkward and uncomfortable.

Norman Miller sat across from her, not too close, making conversation in an attempt to bridge the gap between them. They'd had bright hellos and hugs on the school steps, and small-talk in the cab. Julie was wondering when he was going to get around to it.

'Breakfast at the airport in Detroit,' her father mused, toying with his chef's salad, 'luncheon at the Summer Terrace in Manhattan. Talk about culture shock.'

Julie smiled, but it was a strained effort. Norman Miller could see as much.

'School's going okay?' he asked.

'Okay,' Julie said. And then; 'Better than okay. But it just seems silly to be talking about school and breakfasts and . . . anything but what it is you came all this way to tell me.'

He smiled a little lamely, and took a small sip of his wine. 'Growing up on me, aren't you?' he said.

'Trying.'

'Well, then, I'll stop beating about the bush.' He set down his glass, and got serious. 'There's a time between a parent and child - maybe more between a father and a daughter - when the daughter looks upon the father as darn near perfect. A king. Daddy can't do anything wrong. No mistakes possible. And part of growing up . . . a sad part, maybe . . . is when you find out that's not so. That old Dad is just as capable of fouling up as the next person. Such as the way I fouled up what your mother and I had.'

He seemed to be fighting with something very difficult. Julie was with him all the way, willing him to come through; he seemed to sense this, but the job didn't get any easier.

'Growing older doesn't mean that a person makes fewer mistakes,' he went on, and then he gave her a rueful smile. 'We just feel a lot sillier when we make them.'

'But what mistake . . .'

'Maybe mistake isn't the right word. It's just important that you understand that grown-ups can get confused, too.'

She was starting to get impatient, now. 'Daddy, I'm not following you.'

'What I'm trying to say is that making a mistake doesn't mean a person can't start fresh, to try to put things right again. To rebuild. You follow me so far?'

'I hope so.'

She really hoped so.

★

Doris caught up with Julie between classes, later that afternoon. They had only a couple of minutes before the start-of-session bell, but Doris was popping with eager anticipation.

'*Nu*?' she said. 'Well?'

'You want the good news or the bad news?'

'You know me; I want it all.'

'The good news is, you were right. My father wants to get married.'

Doris would have jumped, but tides of people in a hurry were pushing them from both sides. 'Didn't I tell you!' she said. 'The same way with my...'

'The bad news is, the lady he's going to marry is not my mother.'

Doris felt as if she'd suddenly been dumped in cold water.

But then Julie probably wasn't feeling so hot, either.

'... So when he said he was getting married,' she told Shorofsky bleakly, 'it just brought up all those old feelings. And the harder I fought to keep them inside, the harder they fought to get out. And I'd built up such hopes that...'

Julie shrugged, her voice trailing away. She felt as if she was just talking around and around in circles, getting nowhere and making no real sense.

Shorofsky nodded as he listened. He'd moved over

to stand by the window, to take the pressure off Julie so that she could speak or lapse into silence, whatever she wanted. She'd come to him on the pretext of wanting to discuss the orchestra parts for the Festival of Musical Arts – no more than a couple of weeks away now, with the posters on show around the Lincoln Centre by the park and the tickets already on sale – but it had soon become obvious that there was something else on her mind.

He looked out. Forty-Sixth was quiet, but the Avenue of the Americas at the end of the block was a solid mass of unmoving cars, most of them in the bright yellow livery that was a requirement for all New York City cabs. People were leaning on their horns, and further down the block a siren was howling as a police car or ambulance struggled in vain to get through.

'Lots of trouble out there,' he mused. 'Lots of pain.'

Julie looked at the floor, and Shorofsky turned his back to the window and began to pace.

'You know, Miller,' he said, 'every composer worth his salt knew about pain. Very few were what you or I would call "happy". But they took the pain, as well as the joy, and put all of it into their music.' He stopped pacing, and glanced at her. 'In case I'm not being obvious enough, that's a hint.'

'That's the problem, Mister Shorofsky. I'm scared that maybe I don't have any music left in me.'

He confronted her. 'There will always be music inside of you, Miller. *This* I guarantee.'

She stood up, and looked at him for a long and

hopeful moment. Then, before she knew it, she was hugging him.

'Miller,' Shorofsky said, wincing slightly at the pain in his neck, 'you're a cellist, not a chiropractor. Please let go.'

She backed off at once, with an embarrassed smile. Shorofsky groped around for an exit line, couldn't find one, and then made a somewhat redfaced exit anyway.

But Julie wasn't sorry. Not a bit of it.

18

Shorofsky didn't get to see much of Julie during the next two weeks. She was there in class and she was there at the orchestra rehearsals, but she kept herself back as just another student in the crowd. He couldn't help wondering how she was getting along with her difficulties, but he knew better than to ask. An excess of interest from outside wouldn't help her now; it would only distract her and slow down the process of healing . . . assuming that a process of healing was taking place.

Even if Shorofsky had believed otherwise, he had other things on his mind; however responsible he felt towards the difficulties of any of his individual students, he was also aware of his responsibility to the student body as a whole. As always there was a lot to do, and seemingly insufficient time to do it in.

Troy was the least of his worries. The strong support of everybody in the school had given him the confidence that he needed, and the Chase School for the Educationally Handicapped had booked a block of tickets for students and their families that promised an even stronger turnout than the one Martin Gish had been able to muster at the scholarship finals. It was hard *not* to feel confident when your backup contingent outnumbered everybody else, performers and theatre staff included.

As for the orchestra, they read up on their parts and came prepared to rehearsal just like any set of professional musicians turning up for a concert or a recording date. They meshed almost from the first moment that Shorofsky raised the baton; his was the job of leading them through, adjusting, encouraging, standing back from the work as a whole and giving them the feedback that they needed. It was a pleasure to survey them, none of them past their teens, all relaxed in their concentration. Moments like these were what made Shorofsky's teaching career worthwhile.

Nights like the one on which the Festival was booked to take place, however, sometimes made him question it. The early evening skies had opened, turning the sidewalks into splashing mirrors and the gutters into sluices. Shorofsky sheltered in the entranceway to the Sixty-Sixth Street subway station, watching for a cab and telling himself that he had no chance. Whenever it rains, all the cabs go and hide somewhere - everyone knew that, even though Bruno Martelli often insisted in his father's defence that it wasn't true. Martelli said that the drivers just put their flags up and then cruise around laughing at all the cheapskates who gave them quarter tips in the fine weather. As ye sow, so shall ye reap.

In the end, Shorofsky decided to run for it. The

rain wasn't letting up, but it was only a block or so. The original plans had been for the Festival to be held in the Allice Tull hall in the Juillard School attached to the Lincoln Centre, but as the event had developed and become more ambitious in scope they'd had to rethink their plans and relocate in the larger and more prestigious Philharmonic Hall across the way. The decision had pleased Shorofsky; it would be a good experience for his students to share a venue with the Metropolitan Opera Company and the New York State Theatre. He only hoped that the Met could stand the competition.

Shorofsky would never have passed the auditions for *Chariots of Fire*. Although his conducting tails were safe in a zippered nylon suit bag that he kept close under his arm, he arrived backstage feeling as if he'd taken a shower with all his clothes on. There was no great rush - the school's contribution was scheduled to open the second half of the programme - but he wanted to be there and available from the earliest moment.

But he couldn't move without squelching. He couldn't raise his arms without splashing more water onto the floor.

'Mister Shorofsky,' Julie said from behind him, 'you're soaking wet!'

He turned, smiling patiently. He hadn't needed to be told. 'It's pouring with rain out there,' he said.

Julie seemed surprised. 'It is?'

She must have been here for an hour or more already. She was in her long, simple concert dress and wearing a touch of makeup. She looked... better. Shorofsky couldn't be annoyed. He said, with a wink, 'And they were lined up for blocks.'

For a moment Julie didn't understand, but then she remembered the reassurance that he'd given her after the scholarship finals. *Put Julie Miller in the music, and they'll be lining up for blocks.* She looked away sheepishly, but it wasn't real embarrassment.

Shorofsky knew that if he didn't get towelled off and changed, he was going to get pneumonia. He was too *busy* to get sick. But as he was about to go on to the dressing room complex, he remembered something.

'Is he here?' he asked Julie.

She knew who he meant. 'No,' she said, 'he isn't.'

'He had to go back to Michigan?'

'I didn't invite him.'

It wasn't what he'd expected to hear. 'I thought we agreed on this. The music is for sharing.'

'I know you say that a lot . . . and maybe you're right when you tell me the music's ready. But there's only one person who can say when *I'm* ready, and that's me.' And then, with decorous politeness; 'I mean, I don't have to follow all your advice all the time, do I?'

He had to laugh. His clothing was soaked through and every time he moved it was like cold sponges were being squeezed out under his shirt, but he had to laugh.

'Miss Miller,' he said, 'for such a young girl, you are quite a young lady.' And he took her right hand

and kissed it lightly. 'And now I have rosin in my beard,' he said.

In the dressing-room corridor, he found Troy Phillips.

Troy was sitting on a cane-backed chair and reading a Spiderman comic book, not one of the special remedial reading editions but the real thing. He looked up as Shorofsky came by; he seemed calm, relaxed, ready for anything.

'Well, Troy,' Shorofsky said. 'How does it feel?'

Troy thought it over for a moment. 'Like it's showtime, Mister Shorofsky,' he said.

19

The Festival report in the *Daily News* made a point of mentioning Troy Phillips by name. Angelo Martelli found it first and hurried up to Bruno's bedroom, throwing the folded paper onto the bed and then opening the drapes to let the morning sun come flooding in. Bruno howled with pain and disappeared under the covers, re-emerging inch by inch as the realisation that he was awake slowly took hold.

It was Saturday, so no school, and it was almost ten. Bruno dressed quickly in T-shirt and jeans, and after rubbing the sleep from his eyes he took the newspaper down to the kitchen. Angelo told everybody that his boy only worked on quarter-power for the first hour of the day; he'd never be able to find the kitchen at all if it wasn't for the scents of coffee and waffles leaving him a trail.

With the Bugs and Roadrunner show playing with muted sound on the kitchen TV, they sat in the breakfast nook and Bruno read the whole piece aloud. His song got a good mention, although the title wasn't given and he wasn't actually named as the composer; the best part of it was given over to an appreciation of Troy's contribution. Bruno read with a mixture of pleasure and apprehension; the apprehension proved to be unfounded, because nothing was said of Troy's involvement with Chase or of his 'special' educational needs. Troy had made it, and on the only terms that counted.

Bruno couldn't help wondering what Coco would think of this. If Troy had never happened along for an audition, it was generally agreed that the lead spot would have been hers. As it was, she'd sung backing and harmonies; she'd handled both with good grace, but nobody had needed to ask if she was really happy.

All the same, the piece gave Bruno a good feeling. After he'd given Angelo back his paper, he said, 'You know what I think I'll do?'

'You're going to go down into the basement and mess around on your synthesizer,' Angelo said without even looking up.

'You got it,' Bruno said, and he dropped two more frozen waffles into the toaster and drew off some more coffee to keep him going.

Bruno went downstairs, switched on the lamps, and warmed up the ARP. There might have been better ways of spending a sunny Saturday afternoon, but Bruno didn't know any. He left the basement door open, knowing that Angelo liked to be able to listen as he messed around the house; when there was heavy work and deep thinking to be done the door would be closed by mutual agreement, but for now Bruno was just 'futzing', as Shorofsky would say, with a few chord sequences. It was like a writer jotting in his notebook, or an artist on his sketchpad; from the free-form wandering, an idea might emerge.

Around mid-afternoon, Angelo put his head around the door.

'Bruno,' he said, 'you got a visitor.'

'A visitor?'

Angelo opened the door all the way, and Doris Schwartz came down the stairs into the basement.

'Hope this isn't an interruption,' she began, but Bruno quickly reassured her.

'No,' he said, 'just . . . just kicking a few ideas around. You know.'

There was an awkward silence, and then Angelo said, 'I'll go make some popcorn.'

Doris said, 'Oh, none for me, Mister Martelli, thank you,' and Bruno started to say the same, but Angelo was already on his way up the stairs and closing the door behind him.

Bruno could see that there was something troubling Doris, but it hardly seemed right to come straight out and ask what it might be. If she wanted him to listen, he'd listen; but if she didn't, and if she got some other comfort just by being here, then that was fine. He thought back to the last time that they'd been like this, here amongst all the equipment on what his father sometimes called the bridge of the Starship Enterprise. Doris had come around then because Bruno had asked her to; he'd got himself tangled up in an awful net of crossed loyalties and unwanted responsibilities when he'd accepted an invitation from Dave Reardon to sit in with the all-staff production team for the staging of his first short musical.

She'd helped him then, and it seemed that she needed help now. Bruno thought that he might have an idea why.

'I got a favour to ask,' Doris said.

'Name it.'

'Can I stay here for tonight?'

'Sure.' There were two spare bedrooms in the Martelli house; no problems, and no cheap rumours. 'You want to talk about it?'

But Doris shook her head. 'No. I just want to say one thing. I hope you know how lucky you are; to have what you have with the guy making popcorn upstairs. I know it's just you and him, but it's family.'

'I know,' Bruno said. He also knew for sure now the root of Doris's trouble. Her brother Marty had been away for four and a half years, but now he was back in town. The tough part was that her father wouldn't have him in their house or even speak to him. Marty's fast disappearance from the city had come about with the arrival of his draft papers through the mail; rather than accept the army's invitation to Indochina, Marty had invited himself across the border into Canada where he'd made his way as a theatre lighting director. Amnesty had taken the price off his head, but it seemed that amnesty stopped at the Schwartz front door.

Bruno dug around through the sheet music on top

of his electric piano. He found a particular hand-written score, and slid it across to Doris.

'You ever hear me play this?' He started in on the keyboard.

Doris nodded. It was something that they'd been hearing around the school for weeks now, a Bruno Martelli original, although he'd never officially played it for anyone to hear. They'd get snatches of it coming from an empty auditorium, or through the closed door of one of the practice cubicles.

The door opened again and Angelo came through, a bowl of super-quick popping popcorn under his arm. He came over, and set the bowl down by them.

'Boy,' he said, 'do I ever love that song.'

He sat and listened for a while, until Bruno came to the end. Then he said, 'How 'bout I get us something to drink?'

'Stay where you are, pop,' Bruno said, bouncing up. 'I'll get it.'

He went clattering up the stairs, and Angelo took his place. He looked down at the keyboard. He couldn't have played a note to save his life; he always said that talent had skipped a generation and wound up as a double-dose in his boy.

He said, 'I remember when he wrote that song. Such a fight we were in.'

'The two of you?' Doris said, surprised.

'The worst. Both of us walkin' around not sayin' a word to each other. Silly.'

'What was the fight about?'

'Who remembers? I just remember drinkin' my

coffee black for a week 'cause I wouldn't even ask him to pass the creamer. Finally, somebody had to do something. He came down here and wrote that song. Cut right through all the other stuff.'

'But you did something too,' Doris suggested.

'I did?'

'You listened.'

Angelo thought it over for a moment. 'Yeah. I guess I did. It wasn't hard.'

Doris looked at the carpet. Angelo said, 'You okay?'

'If I asked you to give me a hug right now... a fatherly hug... what would you say?'

'I wouldn't say a thing,' Angelo said, and he wrapped his arms around her. Doris screwed her eyes shut, and hung on tight.

It was going to be all right. But sometimes you just needed a little help to carry on.

20

Doris's move paid off, but not in the way that she'd expected.

She gave the news out in edited snatches during dance class, to anyone who showed an interest and to a few who had other things on their minds. It seemed that the message she'd left for her parents - that she'd be staying overnight with Bruno and his father down in Queens - hadn't made it through; distracted with worry when the early morning came and she still hadn't shown, her own father had gone straight to brother Marty's loft in Greenwich village in the hope that he'd find her there. Doris actually came along a half-hour after he'd arrived, to find the ice broken and a reconciliation in the making.

'Yeah, great news,' Danny Amatullo told her, although in truth he was only listening with one ear; the rest of him was trying to keep focus on what Lydia Grant was saying. Most of today's exercises so far had involved boy-girl pairs, and Danny was wondering if it would be possible to work his way across the group so that he could end the session in a *pas de deux* with Dee Wilson, a cute little redhead whose leotard appeared to have been spraycanned onto her body by a Playboy centrefold retoucher.

But before he even knew it, he was paired with Doris Schwartz.

'The point of any lift,' Lydia Grant explained as she walked down between the two facing lines of dancers and would-be dancers and actors out to stretch their range, 'is to mask the effort. The audience doesn't want to see how hard you're working. As far as they're concerned, you're all as light as feathers.'

'Auntie Em,' Doris piped in her best Judy Garland voice, 'we're not in Kansas anymore...'

'Doris,' Lydia reassured her, 'you are going to be as light as a feather.'

'Don't tell her,' Danny protested, 'tell me. I've got to lift that feather, and I think I'm going to need a truss as big as the Bronx.'

The line got a laugh, as Danny's lines almost always did, and when he glanced down the line he was gratified to see that Dee Wilson was smiling along with all the others. What he didn't notice was that Doris's smile was a little forced, a little glassy.

Lydia raised her voice as the laughter trailed away. 'All right, now,' she said as she reached the end of the line and picked up her dance staff, 'that's enough. Let's have the first pair.'

She rapped out a cadence with her staff on the floor, and the first pair moved out. They executed a lift that wasn't bad, but nothing special. The next pair was better, the third pair wobbled. The fourth pair was Leroy and Coco; Leroy lifted like his hands were empty, and Coco flew.

'All right,' Lydia commented, 'looking good. Next pair.'

Doris was doing her best to get into feather feeling mode, but she wasn't exactly happy about it. The cadence of Lydia's staff was like a countdown. The truth was that Danny's remark had hurt her, just a little - although if she was going to be really honest with herself, it went a lot deeper than that.

Their turn arrived. Danny's expression didn't help; it was nothing personal, he just hated to dance. It was a non-optional part of the drama course, so he couldn't do as Bruno had done and duck out.

They met, and Danny grabbed a couple of painful handfuls of Doris and lifted. To begin with, their timing was out; if Danny's lift had meshed with Doris's leap, they'd have made it through. But he treated it like a stevedore, with Doris as the cargo, and he got her waist up to shoulder height and then found he could go no further.

Doris was trying to think like a feather, but events had gone pretty much beyond her control. Danny took a staggering step, refusing to give up so easily, and tried to complete the lift.

He might as well have quit, having established the principle that all grace was milked out of the move when the female half of the team was treated and hoisted like a barbell, but he didn't. Gravity had to do the job for him.

If this had been a drama class, and the exercise

had been an enactment of the falling of the walls of Jericho, then they'd have scored top points. As it was, the end-of-session bell saved Lydia from having to make any comment.

'Bless you, bell!' she shouted over the ringing. 'Showers, everybody! Move it!'

Everyone headed for the piano and the barre to collect their gear and towels, except for Danny and Doris who took a little longer to untangle themselves on the floor.

'That wasn't my fault!' Danny insisted from somewhere underneath.

'Why wasn't it?'

'You were all sweaty. I couldn't get a good grip!'

Doris got to her feet and went over to the barre. The fall had given her normally buoyant spirits a slow leak.

Coco was stuffing a pair of legwarmers into her tote bag. She saw Doris approaching in the full-length dance mirror, and could tell without much difficulty that the spirits of Mrs Schwartz's little girl had taken a definite down.

She said, 'Don't worry, Doris. You'll get it.'

'Easy for you to say,' Doris said as she reached for her mopup towel. 'Can you give me any tips or hints or anything?'

Coco shrugged. 'Maybe one thing. Don't be so... easy on yourself. Pick a direction and go all the way with it.'

'That's fair,' Doris said, wondering what the hell Coco was talking about. 'Anything else?'

Coco smiled a little regretfully, and slung the tote bag over her shoulder. 'I can't now, Doris. I've got to meet Bruno for a phone call.' And with a little wave she was gone, leaving Doris to wonder if communal telephoning was about to become the school's new vogue with Coco and Bruno in the *avant-garde.*

Coco's place was taken by Danny Amatullo. He was holding out his hand to shake. He said, 'Truce?'

Doris considered it. 'Well,' she said, 'if you're dropping me when we're on a friendly basis, I suppose I don't want to know what would happen if we became enemies. Truce.'

They shook hands and then together they headed out into the hallway, towels looped over their shoulders. Danny took a quick look over the crowd in the corridor but Dee Wilson had already gone, disappeared to that faroff land beyond the place where sea and sky meet and where the things that we know would make us happy live just out of reach. Or else she'd gone to the showers. What difference did it make?

'You see Leroy and Coco?' Doris said as they pushed their way through the crowd to get a look at the bulletin board. 'How come they make it look so easy?'

'They've got an unfair advantage,' Danny said. 'They're dancers.'

'Coco's got an unfair advantage in everything.'

'Can't imitate Coco. You've got to do it your own way.'

A group moved from in front of the board, and

they slipped into the space. Apart from the usual warnings about locker-room thefts and study hall discipline, most of the board was given over to notices concerning shows-in-production or else auditions and rehearsal calls.

'Look at this,' Doris said, shaking her head. Wherever she looked, the same name seemed to catch her eye. 'She's in everything, and I'm playing a dead body in a murder mystery.'

'Will you cut it out?' Danny said. His annoyance was mostly faked. 'So what if she got a few parts? It's just coincidence.'

'You're very sweet, Amatullo - and very naïve. Coco's got what you call "halo effect". Ever hear of it?'

'No, but I'm about to.'

'When you do something really well, it kind of slops over into everything else you do. It's like having a bright halo around your head. So I can't just be as good as Coco - I have to be better. And that's what I intend to do. She's had it easy long enough.'

Doris turned and walked away, with new resolve. *Oh, no,* thought Danny. *This is going to mean trouble for somebody. I only hope it isn't me.*

21

As fast as Coco ran, Leroy still got to Bruno before her. The only difference was, Leroy didn't know that he was in a race. Coco watched the two of them at the top of the stairs, hopping impatiently and trying to look as if she wasn't. Finally Bruno nodded, Leroy clapped him briefly on the shoulder, and they separated.

Bruno came down to join Coco, and together they headed for the pay phones in the lobby. Bruno lined up the change, and Coco unfolded a torn-out page of *Variety* with the crucial telephone number ringed several times in red.

'It's all there, Bruno,' she said, 'everything you need to know,' and Bruno nodded and smiled and tried to calm her down a little.

He was kept on hold for nearly three minutes before he was put through. Without wasting any time, he got straight into it.

'I'm Miss Hernandez's theatrical representative, and I was wondering if you had time to see her this afternoon?' He turned in the booth, and gave Coco a reassuring wink. 'Well, I'm not at all sure whether or not she'll read. I just assumed you people would want to see her for the part.'

Coco gestured frantically; Bruno was overplaying

his hand. Read for the part? She'd grovel for it if she had to. But Bruno was beginning to enjoy himself.

'Of course I'm with the William Morris agency. My name's . . .' a fractional hesitation ' . . . Rosselli. Marty Rosselli. The reason you haven't heard of me is that I just transferred here from L.A., so I'm semi-new to New York.'

He looked at Coco again and started to make an *okay* sign with finger and thumb, but it died halfway. 'Hello? Hello?' He shrugged, and put the receiver back on the cradle with exaggerated delicacy. 'I guess we were cut off.'

It seemed more likely that the casting director's first assistant knew a snow job when she heard one, but neither of them said it out loud. Coco was disappointed, but no less determined.

'Bruno,' she said, 'I'm so right for that part, it hurts. I totally understand the character of Angela. You know I saw *Cakewalk* six times? I cried every time Angela had her big scene.'

'What can I say? Life isn't fair. It's their loss.' Looking at Coco, Bruno was dissuaded from any further attempt to dismiss her feelings. He said, 'Come on over to my place after school. Leroy just asked me if I'll help him work on his showcase. The sounds will cheer you up.'

'Well . . .' Coco managed a smile. 'Only if it's okay with Marty Rosselli at William Morris. He's my agent.'

★

Putting a tape together for Leroy offered a good opportunity for Bruno to use his latest gadget, an attaché case-sized studio setup that had started its life on an assembly line in Tokyo and found its home in the Martelli basement. Using the full width of a cassette running at half-speed, it gave him four channels of mixing with Dolby circuits giving every repeat run a first-generation sound. Leroy had some pre-recorded music that he wanted blending into a single sequence with no obvious edits. It was an ideal challenge for the equipment.

Leroy walked through his steps in a cleared area in the middle of the basement, counting softly under his breath. Bruno had a rough idea of what he was going to do - vary the speed of a couple of the tracks to make the rhythms match, and unite the whole sequence with an extra percussion underscoring - but it helped to see what Leroy was hoping to achieve.

Leroy, for his part, had welcomed the idea of having Coco along to watch and give advice. But although Coco was indisputably there, it seemed that her mind was off taking a walk somewhere else.

'Girl,' Leroy said, 'I get more enthusiasm from my eighty year old grandmother. And she's been dead for two years.'

'What is it?' Bruno said, as the upstairs door banged back and footsteps came down towards them. 'Still on the audition?'

'I just can't shake it,' Coco admitted.

'Well,' Leroy said, 'can you at least try? This may just be a project to you, but it's *my* semester showcase.'

Bruno's father came backing into the basement, carrying a tray with a tall pitcher of Kool-Aid and four glasses. 'It sounded very thirsty down here,' he said.

Bruno went over to help with the tray. 'Good timing, pop,' he said, no pun intended. 'I think we're taking a break anyway.'

Leroy muttered something dark that nobody was supposed to hear, but he accepted a glass of soda with thanks and moved apart to think his routine through while the others sat and chatted.

Angelo said, 'So, how's it going?'

'Ask Coco,' Bruno advised, and Coco looked at the floor with some embarrassment. 'You know,' Bruno went on, 'personally, I don't think *Cakewalk* is going to make a very good flick anyway.'

Coco promptly forgot her embarrassment. 'How can you say that? With Charles McKay directing? He's a genius.'

'Maybe, but when you put a closed-in show like that up on the screen, it dies.'

Coco almost seemed to take the criticism personally. A group of them had gone to see the show on a block discount booking, and the next day Coco had been waiting for three hours when the ticket booth in Times Square opened for business. She was only fourth in a line that stretched a block and a half. Not only did she re-book then, but she kept going back every few weeks as long as the show was running on Broadway. And then there was Charles McKay; a dancer turned choreographer turned movie director, he'd trodden a path of success that put him right up there in Coco's gallery of showbiz heroes along with Herbert Ross and Bob Fosse.

She said, 'I'm sure he knows the problems and he'll do something to fix them. The important thing is that *Cakewalk* has got heart.'

'That's just what *he* said,' Angelo Martelli agreed, nodding.

Bruno felt as if he'd missed out on a piece of the conversation. 'Who?'

'McKay.'

Coco couldn't believe it. '*Charles* McKay?'

'I gave him a ride the other day. Real nice guy. He said he puts a lot of stock in what regular people think about his movies. Anyway, I told him I never saw *Cakewalk*, so he told me about it. He said it had real heart.'

Coco gaped for a moment, her mind working overtime. Then she said, 'How much stock?'

Angelo didn't understand.

'How much stock,' Coco persisted, 'does he put in regular people's opinion? Enough to take your idea about who to cast in the part of Angela?'

'Coco!' Bruno protested. 'He gave the man a ride in his cab. McKay's not going to cast the second lead in his movie on my pop's say-so.'

'I know that. But all I need is a chance to show what I can do.' She turned to Angelo. 'All you'd have to do, Mister Martelli, is tell him you know a very talented young actress who'd be perfect for the part, then leave the rest to me.'

Angelo squirmed a little, but he had nowhere to back off to. 'I don't know,' he said, 'I'd feel kind of funny doing something like that. And besides – chances of me hooking up with him a second time…'

Coco suddenly seemed to realise that she was being too pushy. She backed off, hoping that she'd caught herself in time to prevent any real damage being done.

'Yeah,' she said, crestfallen. 'Yeah, I didn't think about that side of it.'

Angelo thought it over for a few moments, and then said, 'You know Edelstein's Deli?'

Coco thought for a moment. Edelstein's Deli. It was somewhere on West Fifty-Fourth, close to the Twentieth Century-Fox office annexe. When she'd been around eleven or twelve years old, Coco had spent some long hot days in the summer vacations walking around the group of city blocks that housed the Fox offices and the CBS building in the hopes of being spotted on the sidewalk and 'discovered'. She'd stood out in plain sight doing her best to look mysterious and charismatic as she contemplated some inner tragedy, but nobody had ever rushed across the street with a contract. She had, however, come away with a knowledge of every coffee shop and deli in a five-block radius.

'Edelstein's Deli,' she said, 'yeah, I know it,' and

for a moment Angelo looked surprised.

'Well,' he said, 'when I took McKay to his office, he stopped off there for a Danish and coffee. Said he does the same thing every morning. If you just happened to be there, say, around nine in the morning, maybe you could introduce yourself.'

The wheels were starting to spin again. 'That's a fantastic deal!' Coco said, and she bounced up and started to collect her stuff. 'Thanks a lot!'

A moment later, she was running up the basement stairs.

Angelo sat rocking, as if he couldn't believe it. 'Is she always like this?' he asked Bruno.

'Always,' Bruno confirmed, and then he set his glass aside and turned, businesslike, to the tape deck. 'Okay,' he said to Leroy, 'Let's just run it through and see how it all falls together.'

22

Fifteen minutes before the next day's drama class, Danny Amatullo went into one of the dressing rooms looking for an out-of-the-way place to leave his books and his lunch bag. He found Doris sitting before one of the mirrors and doing facial exercises. She was rolling her shoulders, making pop-eyed faces, and flopping her tongue around like a windscreen wiper whilst making guttural noises.

'If I wanted to watch Godzilla eat Tokyo,' Danny said, 'I'd go to the movies.'

'Do I laugh when you do a warmup routine?'

'No. That's the problem.'

'Never mind,' Doris said, turning around on the makeup stool. 'Okay, now really focus and tell me what you see. Lady Macbeth. Ready?'

'Ready.'

Doris launched into her Lady Macbeth from a class exercise of three weeks before.

'That Lady Macbeth had some mouth,' Danny commented when she'd done.

'Danny! What did my body say? Did you see Lady Macbeth or just me?'

Danny considered for a moment. 'You looked like Doris, doing funny things with her body.'

Doris gave up. She took another look at herself in the mirror; a good and searching look.

'Who am I trying to kid?' she said. 'I'm a round, soft-edged Jewish girl, not a murderous queen. Even Coco looks more Scottish than I do.'

'Doris, you look fine.'

'But I don't *feel* fine. I feel like a walking Twinkie. A large family-sized falafel. How am I supposed to move gracefully on a set of thunder thighs?'

'Doris,' Danny began, but Doris was no longer listening. She marched over to the table where she'd left her bag and her overcoat. Seconds later a large film-wrapped sandwich was going into the trash can, followed by two Dunkin' Donuts and a bag of M & Ms.

Danny said, 'Now what are you doing?'

'I'm getting rid of anything in here that's fattening,' Doris said with determination, messing everything up in the trash can so she wouldn't be tempted to fish it out again.

'Doris, it won't help.'

'You wanna bet?'

'Yeah. That was *my* lunch.'

'You want us to do *what*?' Leroy said. He was standing with his arms folded, listening skeptically to the plan that Coco was trying to outline, whilst around them were gathered the others of the dance class that Coco had persuaded to stay after school.

'Well,' Coco said, 'don't act so surprised. Dancers

dance, no matter where they are.'

'Girl, that's the craziest thing I ever heard.'

'Look, if I just go up and ask him, what good will it do me? I have to show him I've got the moves.'

'Girl, we can't just beam up to the ship. This is *reality*.'

'No it's not,' Coco said, 'It's show business,' and Leroy let out an extended groan. Coco went on, 'Come on, I can't just stand up there alone. But if I had you guys to back me up, it would really look like something.'

'Yeah,' one of the girls said, 'like a dozen fools, instead of just one. And we'd be those fools.'

'And what if McKay likes it? Who knows? We all might get in the movie. They're going to need a lot of dancers.' She looked around, at all of them. 'Come on – the only reason not to do it is that you don't want to look silly, and that's really stupid.'

She'd hit them where they lived. There was a general muttering, and most of it was going her way. Leroy shrugged, going along with the crowd, and Coco decided to press on right away before any minds could be changed.

'Great,' she said. 'Okay, now, I've worked out a few opening moves.' She went over to her cassette recorder. It was a small battery-operated machine of a kind that sold for thirty dollars or less in lots of places down Seventh Avenue; a far cry from the kind of equipment that Bruno could muster, but then there were considerably more mouths to feed in the Hernandez family.

After a count of ten, up came the number that Coco had lifted from the live Broadway-cast album of *Cakewalk*. As the music played, she went through a simple, straightforward routine that she'd spent most of the afternoon devising, as close as she could remember to the original choreography.

As the track ended, she turned off the machine and said breathlessly, 'Well, what do you think?'

Leroy was the first to speak. 'It's tired, girl. You want to impress the guy, not put him to sleep.'

'It seemed to work pretty good like that when they did it on Broadway,' Coco said defensively, and as she spoke she was suddenly aware that the numbers of her audience had been swollen by a total of one.

'Hi,' Lydia Grant said from the back. 'What's happening?'

She was all dressed, and looked to have been on her way home. She must have heard the music coming from the dance studio, and decided to see what was going on.

'Oh, nothing,' Coco said. 'We were just messing around.'

Leroy took a look in the general direction of heaven. 'You can say that again,' he murmured.

Lydia came through to the front of the group. 'Just working something up on your own, huh?'

'Yeah,' Coco agreed. 'Just for the fun of it.'

'Mind if I take a look?'

Uneasily now, Coco went over to the cassette player and rewound the tape. 'Sure,' she said as the cassette squealed its way back, 'why not? It's kind of rough, though. It's a routine to that hot number from *Cakewalk.*' Coco was feeling as transparent as a goldfish bowl as she hit the *play* button and moved back to the centre of the dance studio floor.

Leroy joined her; he'd picked it up pretty well on a single viewing, but the results were still pretty rough. Lydia watched, getting a sense of what they were trying to do. She really hadn't wanted to hang around, but her instinct was to be supportive. Most other teachers had to watch their students making dives for the door when the end-of-session bell rang; Lydia sometimes had trouble persuading her dancers to go home at all. It was like they'd discovered the secret of wingless flight, and they were hooked.

The routine ended, and Coco switched off the machine. Leroy stood back, waiting for the bad news and almost hoping it would set him free.

'It'll take a little work,' Lydia said. 'I can give you a hand, if you like.'

This wasn't what Coco had expected. 'Sure,' she said with sudden eagerness.

'When do you want to have it ready?'

'Tomorrow morning.'

Tomorrow morning! Lydia thought of a thousand other things she ought to be doing.

'Piece of cake,' she said, and she let her bag drop to the floor.

23

By eight fifty-five in the morning, most of the breakfast crowd had cleared from Edelstein's Deli. They left only a couple of misplaced tourists and a few older customers in no particular hurry to get anywhere.

Edelstein had sold out and gone to Florida ten years before, but the name had stayed. The current owner had run a roadside diner in upstate New York before buying the lease and taking over the business. Since coming to the city he'd been robbed once, had his street window broken twice, and had had his best day's business when crowds had gathered on the pavement outside to watch a would-be suicide tottering indecisively on a ledge five floors up. For six hours the leaper had hesitated before allowing himself to be talked back inside, in which time the deli owner had turned over enough profit for his wife to refurnish their entire apartment.

Joe Grabowski reckoned that he'd seen enough of it all to recognise any problem before it actually arrived in his lap.

But he'd never seen anything quite like this.

About a dozen kids came sneaking in like they

were commandos in a war movie. They were boys and girls, alternating like the teeth in a zipper, and as if at a command they spread out and took seats in the booths and at the tables in a way that suggested they were following some floor plan.

Two of them came to the counter; Grabowski noted with some alarm that they were awfully close to the cash register. The girl had a cassette recorder that she put on the counter by her menu.

'Two coffees, please,' Coco said brightly as Grabowski went towards her with his order pad and then she indicated all of the other kids who had followed her in. 'Just coffee for them, too.'

'All of them?' Grabowski said, surprised.

'Yeah. And put it on my check.'

As the owner lined up the coffee cups for filling Leroy sat and drummed his fingers on the counter top. The more he thought about this – and he'd been thinking about it a lot – the more doomed the whole enterprise seemed to be. Coco, however, appeared to think that they couldn't miss.

She nudged his arm. 'That's *him*!' she said in a fierce whisper.

Leroy looked along the counter to the Danish case. He saw a man in his fifties, fairly handsome expensive suit and a sunbed tan. When he looked back at Coco, he saw that she was hiding her face behind her menu.

'You don't have to do that,' Leroy said. 'He doesn't know who you are.'

'I know what I'm doing,' Coco said, and she gave

everybody the standby signal and then hit the *play* button.

Charles McKay was just being handed his regular order, when the roof seemed to blow off the deli.

Coco had wound the volume of the cassette recorder up as high as it would go, and as the first bars of *Bet Your Life It's Me* shook the walls all of the kids leapt from the booths and fell into place behind Coco. McKay, Grabowski, and the rest of the regular customers just stood or sat around with stunned expressions as they suddenly found themselves sitting in the middle of a Gene Kelly movie.

The dancers launched into their routine, Coco launched into the song, and from Bar One the whole deal started to come unstuck.

They bumped, they clashed, they missed cues. It was a bad time to find out that a routine hammered out in a studio couldn't be transferred without preparation and rehearsal to a real-life venue; people and furniture were in the way, and the composition floor was too slippery. Leroy almost took a fall, and someone else got tangled up in the hatstand when they should have been doing a spin. There was just enough time for it to look really bad, before the recorder's batteries started to give out.

The music sagged, it warbled. Finally it ground to a merciful halt, and so did the team.

McKay blinked once, paid for his coffee and Danish, and headed for the door. Coco caught up with him before he got there, leaving the debris of her big chance scattered around the deli behind her.

'Mister McKay,' she said breathlessly, 'I'm sorry, but I couldn't get into your auditions, so this was the only way. We didn't have time to rehearse . . . and I forgot to check the batteries . . . and . . .' Coco realised what she must be sounding like, but she couldn't help it. She'd be sounding like an outright amateur, one of those no-hopers who appeared on cable TV talent shows singing *Feelings* while someone played a Yamaha organ for accompaniment.

'Anyway,' she finished lamely, 'here's my résumé.' She thrust the three stapled sheets of paper into his hand. 'I think I'd be perfect for Angela.'

Charles McKay, dancer turned choreographer turned movie director turned fugitive, finally made it out of the door.

'Know what?' Leroy said as Coco looked forlornly after the disappearing figure out on the sidewalk. 'You were right. You should've kept your face hidden.'

He went out, and the others followed. Fiasco hadn't been the word for it.

And she still had to pick up the check for fifteen coffees.

It would have been wrong to say that Coco's spirits made any fast recovery, but at least by the time that the mid-day break came around she was able to make an appearance in the lunchroom. In the middle of the usual chaos, Coco was an island of silence. Apart from promising Leroy some help with his semester showcase - she could hardly do less, considering what she'd put him through - Coco sat back and let Doris make most of the noise.

Doris had forgone her usual lunch in favour of a brown bag that appeared to contain nothing more than celery stalks. Danny and Julie Miller were seated on either side of her, and she was favouring them with alternating looks of irritation.

'Is it really necessary to flaunt all that food?' she wanted to know.

'We're not flaunting it,' Danny said as he unloaded an apparently bottomless lunch bag, 'we're eating it.'

Doris looked at the tray that Julie had brought from the hot lunch counter. 'From where I sit,' she said, 'it's definitely flaunting. I mean, who has three beef tacos with chocolate pudding?'

'Doris,' Julie said with a stab at tact, 'you might be expecting too much if you think food is going to just disappear. You can't expect the rest of the school to go on a diet with you.'

'Why not? I go on fire drills with everybody else, the least they can do is go on a diet with me.'

Julie shook her head sorrowfully. 'Too bad celery can't have a million calories and chocolate cake have zero.'

Danny said, 'Then she couldn't live without celery.'

The exchange went on, but Coco wasn't listening. One of the music freshmen had stopped by the table with a note for her that had been sent up from the office by Mrs Berg; after unsealing the envelope and reading it through, she simply sat staring at the paper in her hand. Leroy was closest to her, and with no trace of shame he leaned across and read over her shoulder.

Enjoyed the show very much, the note said, *not to mention the chutzpah. If you can act, too, come to my office on Friday and read something for me.* It was signed *Sincerely – Charles McKay.*

Too stunned to speak right away, Coco handed the note around. When she was finally able to find words, she said, 'It worked! It actually worked!'

'Great stuff!' Danny said, and there was a chorus of much the same from the others.

Julie said, 'How does it feel?'

'I don't know . . . wonderful.'

'Aren't you nervous?' Doris wanted to know.

'Nervous?' Coco said. 'No way. This is my shot, it's what I've been dreaming of all my life. I'm too high to be nervous.' She turned to Leroy. 'Come on, Leroy,' she said, 'admit it. You were wrong.'

'I wasn't wrong,' Leroy said. 'We were fools. How'd I know that's what McKay was looking for?'

But Coco was too high to be brought down. She pushed her chair back and stood, suddenly full of purpose and direction. 'I've got to go find Reardon,' she said.

'Hey,' Leroy called after her, 'what about my showcase?'

'Next week!' she called back over her shoulder.

'It's supposed to be ready next week!'

But Leroy was wasting his time. Coco was already out of the room, disappearing through a crowd of new arrivals in the doorway. There wasn't more than a half-second's pause before Doris was on her feet and following.

She managed to catch up before Coco had reached the teachers' lounge; if Reardon wasn't there, at least they'd be able to tell Coco where he was. Getting level, Doris said, 'Look, I know you're in a hurry. But I need you for thirty seconds.'

'Can't it wait?'

'What are you, a bakery? I have to take a number? No, it can't wait.'

Coco could see that Doris was serious. 'Okay,' she said, 'thirty seconds.' Thirty seconds was about the most that she felt she could manage standing still without exploding.

Doris took a breath, and launched in. 'All the rest of us, we screw up sometimes. We think we want one thing and then we think we want another thing. But you – you never lose sight of it. How do you do that?'

It wasn't a question that Coco had ever given any great thought to. She said, 'I don't know. I honestly don't. I just do what feels right.'

'We all do that, Coco, but with you things actually happen. They call it "Halo effect".'

'"Halo effect?"' Coco said. The term was new to her, but it sounded good. Although she wouldn't have wanted to admit it, a secret and ungenerous part of her mind was urging her to look upon this conversation not as a sharing between equals, but as a meeting of celebrity and fan. 'I don't know,' she said. 'Maybe you're right. Things are going good right now.'

'Don't you ever get... lost?'

'Sometimes. Usually I just go to Bruno, and he manages to say something that puts me back in focus.'

To Bruno? Doris had been thinking that she was the only one who leaned on Bruno when times got rocky, but it seemed that she was wrong.

'Thanks for the thirty seconds,' she said. 'Go start the revolution.'

24

There was a mist out over the Hudson River, even though the day was bright and some of the tall blocks in the city behind them were flaring with the late afternoon sun. Liberty was just a vague pastel smear in the distance as they came out of Battery Park and onto the promenade by the old red-and-white firehouse. Doris had been once to the statue, close to her ninth birthday when some cousins had come over to visit from Illinois; Bruno never.

The wide concrete way was almost deserted; of the few people around, most seemed to be killing time until the next ferry to Staten Island. A couple of gulls sat on the rail, staring eagerly at the bag of potato chips that Bruno had almost finished. Doris was trying not to do the same.

'Either you're in charge of your body,' he explained as they walked, 'or your body's in charge of you.'

'Tell that to the Elephant Man,' Doris said gloomily.

'You've got to realign your priorities. You've got to redefine Doris Schwartz.'

'Bruno, I will never be a skinny nun; I have appetites, okay?'

'You're not trying to deal with it. You're just feeling sorry for yourself.'

'Oh, yeah? You'll notice I haven't asked for any potato chips.'

'Good for you.'

'But would you mind if I licked the inside of the bag when you're done?' she said, and then added quickly, 'Joke.'

'Lie.'

'True.'

Bruno dumped the bag in the nearest trashcan. He turned to Doris with his full attention. The truth was that he was rather enjoying himself; it was flattering to be cast as confessor and unpaid analyst.

'Look,' he said. 'You know what imagining is?'

Doris nodded. 'The Pia Zadora School of Drama.'

Bruno waved the joke aside with a shred of impatience. 'You imagine your appetite as a terrible monster. And you imagine your willpower as a battalion of knights on white chargers.'

'Imagine my what?'

'Your willpower.'

'I've heard of the concept, that's about all.'

'You're not helping,' Bruno warned.

Doris squared herself up to make a serious effort. 'Okay. My appetite's a monster, and my willpower is a battalion of white knights.'

They began to follow the curve of the path around the Castle Clinton monument, heading back into the park and towards the city. Bruno said, 'What you do is, try to imagine that battalion of knights attacking that monster. Over and over again. It's a terrible battle, but they're winning. They're driving the monster away. Are you imagining that?'

'I'm trying. It's not easy.'

'You're not trying hard enough.'

'It's always skinny people who pig out on potato chips who say things like that. I'm telling you, this is not easy. My battalion of knights is dodging the draft.'

Doris did her best to make the effort, but it was doomed before she started. As they turned a corner, they almost walked into a hot pretzel cart. Before Doris could leap out of range, Bruno took her elbow and steered her onto the grass and away from temptation.

'Keep thinking,' he said. 'They're attacking the monster. They're winning. The monster is faltering. The monster is retreating.'

'The monster isn't retreating,' Doris said plaintively, 'the monster is going out to dinner.'

'Look back, and you'll turn into a pillar of salt.'

'As long as I've got the salt, I might as well get some fries to go with it.'

Bruno sighed. Leading Doris out of the Valley of the Calories was going to be more of a trek than he'd imagined.

Coco's after-school session with Dave Reardon was, fortunately for her, going rather better.

'Applause, applause,' Reardon said from the back of the classroom as Coco reached the end of Angela's big solo speech from *Cakewalk*. 'It was good. I liked it.'

'Really?' Coco said, lowering the playbook as Reardon switched on the rest of the room lights.

'Yeah, really. You rushed some of the moments at the top, but I put that down to nerves more than anything else.'

'Yeah,' Coco admitted, 'that makes sense.'

Reardon stuck his hands deep in his pockets, and looked at her in a way that was more than a little searching. 'If this is just some kind of class exercise,' he said, 'frankly I don't see what the nerves are all about.'

'I'm not that nervous.'

'Coco,' Reardon said, and his tone said *don't try to treat me like an idiot.*

'Well,' Coco said, casting around in her mind for something that would suit the occasion without giving her big secret away, 'maybe I'm a little nervous because . . . Leroy and me are kind of on the outs, too.'

'How come?'

'Well, I was supposed to help him with a project he's been working on, and I've sort of been concentrating on this.' She shook her head. 'I just think he's maybe like . . . envious, you know?'

Reardon was doubtful. 'Of a classroom exercise?'

'Well,' Coco said lamely, 'sometimes it doesn't take much to get Leroy teed off.'

Reardon looked at her thoughtfully for a moment, and then he went around to his desk to collect his jacket and the evening's paperwork.

'And sometimes,' he said, 'being the new guy around here, I have to tread a little carefully. Like I know how the school feels about you kids going out for professional auditions.' He glanced at her. Coco knew what he was talking about; professional auditions were out. She'd always known it - but next to what she was hoping to achieve, a petty house rule didn't seem to count for much.

Reardon added, 'Teachers read casting call notices, too.'

He was inviting her to open up. But Coco simply said, 'I really want to thank you for your help, Mister Reardon. I truly appreciate it.'

She grabbed her things and was out of the door before he could say anything else.

Reardon looked after her, ill at ease with the exchange and her evasion. It was hard to know what to do - coming down hard on the side of the rules might mean a crushing of her hopes that would undo all of the work that they'd so far done together, whereas a blind eye meant that to some extent he'd be betraying the school.

Perhaps it would be best to let things run their course. One way or the other.

25

Nobody else was waiting to read for McKay on the Friday morning, so Coco guessed that the main readings had already taken place and she was being given an outside shot. After a twenty minute wait, she was taken through into his office.

It was smaller than she'd expected, and her eyes were immediately drawn to the display at the end of the broad, empty desk; three TONY awards, all in a line, plus two smaller statuettes that Coco didn't recognise.

McKay came around the desk to make her feel welcome, but they didn't waste any time with social preliminaries. He didn't mention the scene in the deli, for which Coco was grateful. McKay gave her a copy of the screenplay – it looked strange, a lot different to her playbook – and allowed her to pick her own scene.

She gave him the speech that she'd rehearsed with Reardon, barely glancing at the script because she'd come to know it so well. A couple of lines from the end, McKay said, 'All right, Coco, you can stop there. How did you get to be so good and still not have an agent or any credits?'

She couldn't believe what she was hearing, but a

little warning voice told her to beware of the ego-massage that always precedes the big letdown. She said, 'I go to the School of the Arts. That takes up most of my time.'

McKay thought it over for a few moments. 'Well,' he said, 'we've seen a lot of actresses, singers, dancers . . . some more talented than you, some less . . .'

'Does that mean I've got a shot?'

He made a decision. 'Yes, I'd say you definitely have a shot.'

'When will you decide finally? I mean, I can come back for auditions as many times as you want me to.' She knew that she was starting to gabble, but she couldn't help it.

'I wish it were strictly up to me,' McKay said, 'but I'm afraid it isn't that simple. You'll have to do a screen test.'

They were words out of a dream. 'Have to? I'd *love* to!'

'Now,' he warned, bringing her down, 'this isn't a try-out for one of your school plays or one of your movie fantasies. There are five other girls set for screen tests. So, if you want a chance, you'll have to knock their socks off. Do you understand?'

The reality of the situation had sobered Coco a little. 'I understand, Mister McKay,' she said. 'I'll be ready.'

McKay nodded pleasantly, and moved to show her to the door. 'You leave a number where we can reach you, and we'll let you know when it's all set.'

'Okay, I will. And thank you.'

'Hope it happens for you. And if it does, it'll mean some big changes in your life. Like quitting your school, moving out to the coast.' She seemed to hesitate. 'You are aware you'd have to quit school?'

'Oh, sure,' Coco said. 'I knew that.'

She supposed she'd known it. But why hadn't it really hit her until now?

26

On the Monday morning, Julie reached her locker just as Bruno was dialling out his own combination nearby. She said, 'Have you seen Coco yet this morning?'

'Nope,' Bruno said.

'Did she call you or anything?'

'Yup. I'll let her tell you herself.'

'Oh,' Julie said, disappointed at this lack of hot news. 'She didn't get the part?'

'I didn't say that.'

'She's got a part, but not the one she wanted?'

'I didn't say that, either.'

'She got a walk-on, but with lines?'

'Julie, if you ever get tired of the cello, you'd make a great interrogator for the KGB.'

Julie left her locker to come closer to Bruno, and she lowered her voice conspiratorially. 'I won't tell anyone you told me,' she said.

'Told her what?' Danny Amatullo said over Julie's shoulder.

'About Coco's screen test,' Bruno replied automatically, before he'd even realised what he was saying.

'Wow!' Julie said as Leroy passed behind her. 'A screen test!'

'Hey,' Bruno said quickly. 'Do me a favour and don't get all weird about this. Coco's feeling a little uptight, so don't make a big deal out of it, okay?'

Leroy gave a little whistle. 'Temperamental star already, huh?'

'And she doesn't need that kind of talk, either.'

'You her manager now?'

'I'm her friend, just like you are. So give her a break, all right?'

Danny looked around, helplessly. 'So how are we supposed to react?'

'Calm and restrained,' Bruno advised. 'Normal, if that's possible.'

'But Bruno,' Julie said with barely-suppressed excitement, 'this could be the turning point of her whole career - her whole life...'

She would have gone on, but Danny signalled her to be quiet. Coco was just coming down the locker room stairs.

'Hey,' she called as she came over, 'Bruno tell you what happened?'

'Ah, no,' Julie said. 'He said you'd tell us.'

'They want me back for a screen test.'

Four faces around her smiled pleasantly at the good news. It was the kind of reaction that she might have expected if she'd come back from the dentist with a clean bill of health.

She tried again. 'Isn't that fantastic?'

'That's very exciting, Coco,' Julie said neutrally.

'That's great,' Danny added in the same kind of tone, and Leroy said, 'Real happy for you.'

Coco's look was one of puzzlement, but she covered it over. She had, after all, other things on her mind. She said, 'Well, I know you guys are all dying to hear the details, but I've got to get working on my scene. I'll fill you in later.'

With the *Cakewalk* screenplay tucked under her arm, she gave them a brief wave and headed off down the hall.

Bruno turned a jaundiced eye on the group.

'I think you overdid it just a bit,' he said.

Watching Doris in dance class, Danny started to get worried. It wasn't only that she seemed to have no energy, but when he got close-up he saw that she seemed drawn and ill with dark half-moon circles under her eyes. She drew Leroy as a partner, and Leroy left her standing.

In the mid way rest, Danny got himself beside her. He was right, she looked terrible. He said, 'Doris, what's wrong with you?'

'Nothing,' she said. 'I've never felt better. Light as a feather.'

'What are you on, some crazy diet or something?'

'A diet's when you eat nonfattening food. I've been fasting for the past three days and taking those diet snacks you get in the grocery.'

'You mean you haven't eaten *anything*?'

'Look,' she said, 'I'm fine, really. The important thing is that I've lost four pounds already.'

'Come on,' Danny urged, 'at least eat an apple or

something. I've got one in my locker.'

'No,' Doris insisted, 'I've got a plan and I'm sticking to it. I'll start working my way back onto food in two or three days. I'll just have to stay away from Miss Grant's class until then. I'll be fine, really.' And she giggled, a sound which was anything but reassuring to Danny.

But what could he do? It was obvious that he was talking to a fanatic. White knights and monsters. Whoever won, they sure seemed to be making a mess of the battlefield.

Coco managed to catch David Reardon between classes, and she handed him a half-dozen pages. It was the scene that she'd been given for the test, and the one for which she'd asked Reardon's help in the form of extra coaching.

'It would help if the rest of the play was attached,' he commented, scanning the pages.

Hesitantly, Coco pulled out the rest of the script and handed it over. He looked at the bound screenplay, at the cover with the movie-company logo. 'How did you get hold of this?' he said.

'Well,' she began, 'I have this friend in the crew...'

'Save that, and level with me.'

For a long and uncomfortable moment, Coco searched for the right thing to say. The right thing would have been the truth, but the truth wouldn't come.

She said, 'Hey, if it's too much trouble, we can just forget it.'

'All I want is a straight answer, which you're not giving me.'

'I'm sorry,' Coco said, her guilt beginning to show, 'but if I just came in and said...'

She couldn't finish. Now it didn't really matter; Reardon had guessed all that he needed to know.

He said, 'Is this why you've been letting your other commitments go?'

She nodded. 'Do you understand how important this is to me?'

Reardon sat back. The look he gave her was long and cool and difficult to read. Finally he said, 'Yes, as a matter of fact, I do. That's why I'm probably going to help you. Come by after school and we'll see what we can manage.'

'And maybe a little before school tomorrow?' Coco said eagerly. 'Could we do that, too?'

'Before school?' Reardon echoed.

'I can be here by six-thirty.'

'Six-thirty? Coco, my heart doesn't start beating before seven. Let's take it a step at a time, okay?'

Even without the dawn workout, Coco had a lot to be elated over. Her mind was so out-of-tune with her surroundings that she narrowly missed running into Leroy as she hurried out of the classroom.

'Hey, roadrunner,' he said. 'See you after school.'

'Can't,' she said, still flying high. 'I'm rehearsing with Reardon.'

'What about *our* rehearsal?'

Coco braked, her elation taking a sudden dive. She turned to face Leroy. 'I totally forgot about it,' she said.

Leroy either couldn't believe her, or he didn't want to. 'Coco,' he said simply, 'I've got to be ready in three days.'

'But I just don't have any time with this thing that's coming up. You'll have to find somebody else.'

Somebody else? With three days to go before his showcase presentation? Bruno could say what he liked, but Leroy had been right. Coco was showing just a little too ready to try the temperamental starlet outfit on for size.

'My mistake,' he said, and his eyes held a coldness that chilled Coco like a dark cloud passing over her grave. 'Well,' he said, 'good luck, Miss Diva.'

He didn't turn, he didn't walk away.

Coco had to do that part all on her own.

Compositions were being returned in Elizabeth Sherwood's English class. Danny watched his paper slowly making its way down the row towards him, regarding it with some apprehension.

'On the whole,' Sherwood was saying, 'you did pretty well this time. Although some of you might look up the word "plagiarism" for future reference.'

'Why don't you just tell us what it means?' Danny said, turning his paper over for a look at the grade and preparing himself for a mental *ouch*.

Sherwood focussed on hm with a grim gleam in her eye. 'It means,' she said, 'in general, that I prefer to read what you think about your subject, rather than what Woody Allen thinks.'

'Oh,' Danny said. 'But how come I got a B-plus *and* a D-minus?'

"The top grade is for grammar and spelling, and the lower grade is for content.'

'I know. So what's wrong with the content of my cousin's wedding?'

'All you talked about was the food. I felt like I was reading an Italian restaurant review. I wanted to know what happened at the wedding.'

Danny shrugged. 'My cousin got married. That's what always happens at weddings.'

Sherwood turned to include the whole of the class in what she was saying. 'I mean how did people feel and act, not the intimate details of how the manicotti tasted or how the lasagna smelled or how moist the rumcake was.' Something moved at the corner of her vision. Doris Schwartz was getting shakily to her feet. 'Doris, what do you think you're doing?'

'I'm just going to get myself a little sip of water,' Doris began, but she kind of ran out of steam halfway.

'Doris,' Elizabeth Sherwood said with concern, 'are you all right?'

Confusion and disorientation suddenly mixed in Doris like explosive gases. 'No!' she almost shouted, 'I'm not all right! I'm too short and I don't have cheekbones and I dance like a rock and there are people in this place who are so damned perfect I can't handle it!'

Sherwood started towards her, but Doris pulled away. She shouldn't have done it, because once she'd started she found with alarm that she had no strength either to stop herself or to keep on standing. She described a perfect arc through the air, and hit the floor like a sack.

'Get the nurse,' Sherwood ordered the boy who was sitting closest to the door. 'Hurry!'

The boy shot out of the room like a cat from under a burning house, and Julie Miller gave Sherwood a hand to raise Doris into a sitting position. Her eyes were open, but she was obviously out.

'Oh, Doris,' Sherwood said, and she smoothed away some of the damp tendrils of hair that were clinging to Doris's pale forehead. 'Oh, Doris.'

Sherwood's face was the first thing that Doris saw when she came around, but it was with a weird kind of effect; the classroom had faded away, to be replaced by somewhere smaller and dimmer and thankfully more quiet.

'You'll do anything to get out of a snap test, won't you?' Sherwood said, and Doris managed a weak smile.

She recognised the place now; she was in the nurse's cubicle, lying on an ancient iron-frame cot with an equally ancient blanket spread over her.

Elizabeth Sherwood reached over to the bedside table, and handed her a small carton of juice with a plastic straw. Doris started to shake her head, but Sherwood wasn't going to let her get away with that.

'You'll drink it or wear it,' she said, and so Doris accepted and took a small sip. It barely tasted of anything at all.

'How long?' Sherwood said.

'Dieting a little over a week. Fasting about three days...'

Sherwood sighed. 'You know, you and I have had some go-rounds in class. When I thought you were being stubborn, and argumentative, and arrogant. But this is the first time I've ever seen you do something that was simply boneheaded dumb.'

'Dumb?'

'Very.'

Doris managed to push herself up a few inches. 'It's always people like you who make speeches like that.'

'You mean teachers?'

'I mean people who are . . . complete. I come to school in the mornings, and you're always so great looking and ladylike and stylish and together – it's like you've got a handle on everything. You know what you're doing and there isn't anything about you that's . . . well, *unfinished*. I know I'll never be like that. I'll never be the kind of lady you are. I'm a schlump.'

'Doris...'

'Hey, come on, let's face the truth. A schlump.' Doris broke off, and took a long pull at the straw in the orange juice container. A sound like a wooden rattle indicated the end of the contents.

Sherwood took the container from Doris, and dropped it in the waste bin on her way to the door.

'Your mother's coming to get you,' she said. 'You're supposed to stay until she arrives.'

Doris nodded. It was no less than she'd expected, and she slid back down under the blanket. Sherwood was about to go, but she stopped with her hand on the lightswitch.

'You know the difference between an adult and a kid?' she said unexpectedly. 'When you come up against something that knocks you for a loop, you think that maybe it hurts so much you'll never get up. But we're older - and we've been knocked down enough by life to know that we almost always can get up. And we also know that we get up just a bit stronger than we were before.'

Doris was about to speak, but Sherwood hadn't finished. She went on, 'Think this over. This so-called stylish and together lady would give her right arm to be half as magical and talented as you are.' She smiled. 'You little schlump.'

And then she switched off the light, and left Doris to her thoughts.

27

When Coco finally got Bruno tracked down, she found that he was in the place that she should have looked first - at the school's second-best piano, the Steinway in the music practice room. He wasn't working, just letting his fingers wander and find their own music. Coco remembered when she'd last seen him like this, working out his problems through a song in the darkened auditorium. He gave her a smile as she came over.

'I just heard about Doris,' she said. 'Is she okay?'

'Okay, I guess. They sent her home with her mom. Where were you all day?'

'Trying to get my scene ready for the screen test. I got the call, it's tomorrow afternoon.'

Bruno could see that she was buzzing with nervous energy, but he said, 'How do you feel?'

'Tired and scared - but all tingly inside, and ready to knock their socks off.'

'Well,' Bruno said, 'everybody's pulling for you,' but Coco thought that there was something not quite convincing in the way that he said it.

'Really?'

'Sure.'

'But there's something else, isn't there?'

Bruno considered for a while. His hands fell silent. He said, 'Look, if this thing happens, you'll have to move on. You'll leave us here.'

'Who says so?'

'Coco,' Bruno explained patiently, 'you'll be a professional. You won't have time for us anymore. You'll have to cut the ties to survive.'

'I'll never forget my friends,' she insisted. 'Bruno, what good would it do me to make it if I didn't have someone to share it with?'

Bruno seemed to think about arguing with her, but then he let it go. The point couldn't be forced, but he knew that Coco would gradually have to come to understand it as the realities of her situation filtered through.

'I don't know,' he said. 'Maybe you should ask Leroy.'

Leroy. She'd already managed to alienate Leroy – how long before the others followed? It felt like a cold knife, deep inside. Was this what it was going to be like? Because if it was, she was no longer so sure that she wanted it.

She shook *that* thought away, and fast. Of course she wanted it, success and everything that came with it; it was what she lived for. Take that away, and her whole life went as well.

Conflict like that could destroy people. So, maybe it *did* happen in showbusiness.

But only to others. Surely, it only happened to others.

28

Coco was late getting in on the morning after her screen test. The appointment had been at the old Astoria Studios across the East River in Long Island City; originally built for the East Coast production of silent movies in 1919, the semi-abandoned buildings had been taken over and refurbished for the production of *The Wiz*. The movie had bombed, but the studio was into a new lease of life. Now everybody was watching for Coco and waiting to hear what the experience had been like. The test was one of the worst-kept secrets in the school's history – although of the staff only Reardon knew anything, and he was staying silent.

Doris was back, and looking better. She took Julie Miller down to Wardrobe with her to sort through some racks of old costumes. Julie asked what had happened after her horizontal departure from Sherwood's class two days before.

'My mother made me go to Doctor Zolen,' Doris explained. 'I hate going to Doctor Zolen. He's known me since I was a baby and he still calls me Dodo. How can a grown man talk like that to a modern woman?'

Julie couldn't help but smile. 'What did he say?'

'First, he gave me a lecture on the four . . . or was it five? basic food groups. Then he gave me a diet that's just dripping with health. He also said I was anaemic. How can a person be pudgy and anaemic?'

'Doris, you just have to be sensible and not go off the deep end with some crazy fad diet.'

'Doctor Zolen told you to say that, huh?'

'No-one told me anything. Like you not telling me what it is we're looking for in all this junk.' She held out one of the costumes, a 1920s flapper dress for somebody with the figure of a shotgun barrel. It looked pretty ratty.

'We're looking for something that will fit me,' Doris said, discounting the flapper dress immediately. 'I sent all my fat clothes to my aunt in Seattle. By freighter. I'll be lucky to get anything back by Christmas.'

Next in line was a shepherdess costume that would have made a hooker blush. Doris was going to make a comment, but a fast lead-in of running footsteps ended in one of the dance class girls bursting into the room.

'Coco just got here!' she said breathlessly. 'She's out in the lobby telling everybody about the screen test! Sounds like it really went well for her!'

She was out of the room again almost before she'd finished; she obviously didn't want to miss a word of Coco's adventures. Julie seemed to vote right along with her.

'Come on!' she said. 'Let's go see what happened!'

'Right behind you,' Doris said as Julie went out

into the corridor. Julie was in such a hurry that she never noticed that Doris wasn't "right behind her"; in fact, there was nobody following her up to the lobby at all.

There were some class papers to be marked, but for once Benjamin Shorofsky let the work lie on his desk untouched. Instead, he closed the classroom door and went to the record cupboard. There were many symbols that could be said to represent a teacher's life, but to Shorofsky the most telling was the large bunch of keys that he always had to carry; every key opened some drawer, some cupboard, some supply room. He'd promised himself that one day he'd get around to labelling them all, but so far he never had.

He checked the index, and took out a record. Here, at least, there was order; student volunteers classified and indexed every record that was bought in by the school. He took the vinyl disc from its cover, and put it on the turntable of the Education Board-issue stereo. No hi-fi buff would have had the equipment in his home – no flickering lights, no smoked glass, no brushed steel facings with bunches of spaghetti-wire hanging out of the back, just a huge wooden box with a hinged lid housing everything but the speakers – but the tone was sweet and clear, and the large empty classroom added an echo of melancholy that gave a real-world dimension to the recording.

It was a symphony, Gustav Mahler's Tenth. Neglected by so many for so long, Mahler was finally coming to be recognised as a composer with decisive influence on twentieth century music. Shorofsky had first heard the Tenth in London during the mid-sixties; an unfinished work with only the first two movements complete and the rest in sketch form, it had been rendered into a performing version by a British composer.

Shorofsky hadn't played the piece often, but for now it suited his mood. He was feeling disturbed.

What had disturbed him was a sight on the sidewalk north of Times Square, a place that Shorofsky passed most days on his way into school. A man had been sitting with his back to one of the buildings, a man in a long dark coat that was torn and shabby. He'd looked to be in his thirties but he was haggard, his hair longish and matted, his beard thick and dark highlighting the skin that was stretched tight over his cheeks. His eyes had been sunken and hollow, little pits of extinguished fire. The man didn't move, and he didn't speak; he just sat there holding out a piece of cardboard - an opened-out box that he'd probably dug from the trash behind one of the Broadway stores - on which, in uneven writing, were the words *Help me, I am starving*. About half a dozen tourists had been standing before him in silence, looking puzzled; it was as if they felt there was something about the situation they hadn't seen, and that by staring they might perceive it.

But this had been no joke, with a punchline to relieve the buildup; this had been real. There had been about thirty cents in small change on the sidewalk beside him.

It was never hard for a New Yorker to walk on by such sights. Ingenious begging was a small industry in the city; well-dressed young men cruised the main railway terminals with a roll of bills in their pockets, looking for the soft-hearted or the out-of-towner to hit with their story. They were always trying to get home, and only a few dollars short of their fare; they'd show the roll of bills, and suspicion would evaporate while sympathy took over.

With such people around, and a constant chorus of *Can you spare some change*? in the streets, the destitute found that they no longer had any credibility. Shorofsky had walked by without hesitating . . . but those burned-out eyes had stayed with him.

He'd seen them before, many times in wartime newsreels and once, unforgettably, in reality through a double-barrier of barbed wire. There had been no fakery. The man was starving.

And here was Shorofsky, in a regular job, getting old in comparative security, and his answer to the situation was to play some music. Every day, he told his students that art and life were one; art wasn't an alternative version of reality to be preferred because it offered softer options, a more reassuring way of looking at the world. Only bad art did that, and bad art was a lie to be despised.

But what, in truth, was he doing now? Wasn't he treating the music as the bad art that he so often condemned, a massaging of the mind, a soothing of the troubled soul? An escape, when the situation demanded confrontation?

Shorofsky moved to the classroom window as the second scherzo began, and he looked down into the street. Almost eighty years before, the composer had stood like this at the window of his New York hotel suite and watched the passing funeral cortege of a fireman. The slow, muffled drumbeats of the funeral march had brought tears to his eyes; Mahler's own death was only three years in the future, and he was already suffering from the serious heart condition that was to bring it about.

Now the fireman was dust, but the moment of his passing remained in the hammerblow beat of a covered drum in the scherzo. Life is a miracle, it said, and life is frail.

Damn it, he didn't seem to have a handkerchief.

Of all the interested crowd that pressed around Coco, Danny Amatullo was the one who seemed to be most fascinated by the details. He wanted to know *everything* - what, who, when, where, and how - and in the end he was slowing the story so much that the others began to shout him down.

'The hardest thing is doing what they call "hitting your mark",' Coco explained. 'If you're off it by just a little bit, they have to do the whole thing over again because it's not right for the camera.'

'Why not just move the camera?' Danny wanted to know. 'The actor's more important than the camera.'

'Hey, man,' Coco protested. 'I'm not going to tell them how to do their job. Not yet, anyway!'

'But it went well, huh?' Bruno said, and Coco came down a little to be serious again. 'Yeah,' she said. 'I mean . . . it'll be a while before I know one way or the other, but . . . what happens, happens. I think I did okay.'

The start-of-session bell broke up the group, and it was obvious that there was disappointment around; this was as close as any of them had ever been to a big-time experience like a screen test, and they were determined to enjoy it even if the enjoyment had to come second-hand. Coco had to make promises to a couple of latecomers that she'd go over the story again after the class with Reardon. If the demand got any bigger, she was thinking, she could put the show into syndication and retire on the proceeds.

But then she saw that Bruno was watching her.

Out of everybody, he'd stayed fairly quiet. Now he hadn't drifted with the others, but seemed to be waiting for her to say something more.

'What's wrong, Bruno?' she said. 'I've got to get to drama class.'

'I think you know what,' Bruno said quietly, and Coco faltered a little – the first crack in the confident façade that she'd been propping up since she walked into the school a half-hour before.

'I don't want to be late for Reardon's class,' she said finally, and she managed to turn away and leave Bruno behind.

Leroy was doing a fast sprint down the hallway as Coco was crossing to the drama studio, obviously late for a class of his own.

'Hey, Leroy,' she called after him, 'I can help you with your showcase now.'

Without even seeming to slow down or to break his rhythm, Leroy did an about-face and ran backwards for a few steps.

'Marguerite's helping me out,' he called back to her, and in his tone there was neither rancour nor any sense of a putdown. 'Doin' a good job, too.' He wasn't out looking for an argument over being let down; he'd managed to patch the hole, and now his attention had to be saved for the work in hand.

'Good,' Coco said, 'I'm glad,' but Leroy was already out of earshot.

There was an extra feeling of support from the class for Doris as she tackled Lady Macbeth's sleep-walking scene for the second time in the term. It wasn't only a new warmth because of her much talked-about collapse in the English classroom; but Doris had changed her approach, shifted gear somehow, and her reading was considerably better. If Doris Schwartz had discovered some kind of secret, then everybody wanted to get in on it.

'That was good, Doris,' Reardon said a moment

after she'd finished, and the babble around him seemed to suggest that the rest of the group thought likewise. 'That was very good. More importantly, it was a heck of a lot better than last time. What did you change?'

'Well,' Doris began hesitantly, 'you said that it lacked substance last time...'

Reardon smiled. 'Do I really talk like that?'

'No, you were right. And I thought that maybe what I wasn't getting was how guilty Lady Macbeth must feel, and so I started thinking about things that made *me* feel guilty. And I sort of used those things.'

'What kind of things? If it's not too personal.'

But it *was* something personal, Reardon could see it right away by the manner in which Doris began to search for the words. She seemed to be dwelling on whether or not she wanted to get into this.

Reardon decided to take her off the hook. 'Well,' he began, 'the specifics aren't all that important,' but Doris interrupted him.

'No,' she said, 'the specifics *are* important. Because they're about me and Coco.'

There was a stirring in the group. Reardon had noticed before that Coco, sitting at the back, wasn't really giving her attention to the work in hand. He'd been trying to think of some way of getting her concentration without having to be sharp or give her an order, but it seemed that Doris had done the job for him; having heard her own name, Coco was right with them.

The two girls were looking at each other; Doris in control, Coco waiting to hear. Reardon wondered how deep these waters were going to be, and whether he shouldn't call a halt now before they got any further.

But he let Doris go on.

She said, 'I can only look at things from inside me, and from inside me it doesn't seem life is all that fair. And sometimes I watch Coco, and it all seems to come together so easy for her . . . the dancing, the singing, everything. I've got to work at it, really work all the time; and when I heard about her and that screen test, it was like the final thing. I envied her so much, but then I felt guilty about all the bad stuff I was feeling. So I took that guilt apart, and I –'

'I stunk up the joint,' Coco said quietly.

All heads turned towards her. She was still fixed on Doris, seemingly talking to Doris alone. She said, 'Everything I told you about the screen test was a lie. I was awful. It wasn't anybody's fault but mine – I got up there, and I choked.' She gave a bitter little smile. 'The harder I tried, the worse it got. I meant it, what I said before; I stunk up the joint.' She shrugged. 'So much for the "halo effect".'

Reardon watched her, glad that he'd let it go through; glad that he'd helped Coco without discouraging her, glad that she'd taken her shot on her own terms and was coming away from it with dignity and an improved understanding of the professional poise that she would one day surely have.

Of all the students seated around Coco, Julie Miller was the most dumbfounded. She'd hung on every word of Coco's account, lived through every moment of the screen test with her; now she could hardly believe that Coco had been spinning it all as she'd gone along. As far as Julie was concerned, it had been Coco's greatest performance to date, bar none.

'Why didn't you tell us?' she said.

'Because I've got this image,' Coco told her, in reality telling them all. 'I'm supposed to be this perfect person that all these good things are going to happen to.' Suddenly there were tears in her eyes and anguish in her voice; she kept them in check, but she couldn't stop them showing through. 'Well,' she said, 'I'm not always magic! I'm just me and I'm afraid and I don't know why I screwed up and why I lied, except that I just got so afraid of...'

Coco ran out of words, but Doris finished the sentence for her. 'Afraid of not being everything everybody else says you're supposed to be,' she said.

Reardon wound it up there. They had a couple of exercises to end the session, but the real work of the day had already been done. Some of the students went out of the class looking puzzled, and others were downright confused; but they'd all been shown an insight on how to cut through their preconceptions and the outer layers that they didn't even know they had, and it was now up to them to arrive at their own understanding.

There were secrets in acting just as there were

secrets in any other kind of craft, but they were the kind of secrets that were always on open display. Learning lines and saying them didn't make actors, any more than wearing medals made heroes; first you had to go through it, and the real ordeals were all deep inside.

Doris Schwartz and Coco Hernandez had come through, and they'd come through whole. They were on their way.

Reardon could hope for no less for the others.

29

When class ended, Coco didn't join in the usual race to the cafeteria. She needed time to be alone, just a little time to get in touch with the new Coco and to try her feelings on for size. Reardon watched her for a moment before he left, but he decided that he wasn't too worried by what he saw. If Coco wanted to talk, she'd talk. Doris lingered for a while, but they'd both said all that they needed to say.

When Coco went out, the lobby hall was almost empty. Shorofsky was just on his way out of the front doors, pulling on his overcoat and in an obvious hurry to get somewhere. All through the school were the odd, indistinct echoes of a brief time-out from furious concentration.

Even though it was the nearest to a relaxed hour that the school would see all day, the heartbeat of practice and rehearsal went on. Leroy and Marguerite would be working through, putting a polish on Leroy's semester showcase. Bruno would probably drop out of whichever crowd he was with and wander through the music faculty, looking for a piano that didn't have somebody's lunchbox on its lid. Julie had already been seen around studying the list of approved pieces that were available to be played by candidates for the next round of Juillard scholarships.

Friends. The word had never before seemed to have the resonance for Coco that it had now. Bruno had been right; if she'd broken away early she'd have lost them forever, out of the crowd before the crowd was ready to follow. Even if nothing else good had come of her blowing the screen test, she had this fact to be grateful for.

She pushed open the swing doors that took her into the darkness of the school's auditorium. Just like last time, there was someone down in the orchestra pit improvising around on the grand piano; and, just like last time, she didn't have to listen for long to know who it was.

Coco lowered one of the back row's tip-up seats, and sat to listen. She couldn't understand why she didn't feel worse; if anyone had asked her about the consequences of failure on the day before the test she'd have said disaster, end of the world, her whole life down the tubes. But the truth was that the world was still here.

Instead she felt a little tougher, a little stronger, and it was a strength that was tempered with a new humility. Maybe she could be knocked down, but she couldn't be stopped.

And the liner notes! Just *think* of the liner notes!

Enough of this. She was sitting out where the audience belonged, and it wasn't home territory. That piano needed a voice.

She got out of her seat, and made her way down towards the stage.